Fintech, Small Business & the American Dream

"The financial crisis destroyed the traditional small business lending system and left these companies with severely impaired abilities to raise capital and grow. In this book, Karen Mills brings her government and her private sector expertise to bear describing how technology may reinvent the ways small businesses operate and raise capital going forward. Economists, policymakers, and anyone interested in the future of small business will benefit from her insights on how the future of fintech and the small business economy will be inextricably linked."
  —Austan D. Goolsbee, *Professor of Economics at University of Chicago Booth School of Business and Former Chairman of the Council of Economic Advisers*

"Small businesses have been the path to economic independence for millions of Americans. Mills shows how fintech can extend that opportunity to even more."
  —Deval Patrick, *Managing Director, Bain Capital Double Impact and former Governor of Massachusetts*

"Few people have done more over the last decade to help small business owners than Karen Mills. Now, in *Fintech, Small Business & the American Dream*, Mills describes a brave new world for small businesses where technology has made capital more readily available and fintech firms use data to break down old barriers. She provides a refreshingly optimistic look at how innovation can bring about Small Business Utopia where the entire financial life of a small business is transformed in a positive way by new technology. But this is not pie in the sky thinking, Mills lays out a detailed plan as to how we can reach this new promised land."
  —Peter Renton, *Founder of Lend Academy and Chairman of LendIt Fintech*

"This book should be required reading for all policymakers with an interest in entrepreneurship, small business development and economic growth."
  —Keith Morgan, *CEO, British Business Bank*

"As we have documented with data from over a million enterprises, small businesses have low cash buffers and bumpy cash flows. Mills' outstanding book assesses the cost of these stresses to small businesses and creates a new vision for technology-driven solutions of the future."
  —Diana Farrell, *President and CEO of JPMorgan Chase Institute*

"Small businesses are often referred to as the 'backbone of the economy' and they need capital to grow and succeed. Mills understands small businesses through her work at the SBA and gives us real insights into how technology will affect, as well as benefit their future."
  —Mike Cherry, *National Chairman of the U.K. Federation of Small Businesses*

Karen G. Mills

Fintech, Small Business & the American Dream

How Technology Is Transforming Lending and Shaping a New Era of Small Business Opportunity

palgrave
macmillan

Karen G. Mills
Harvard Business School
Harvard University
Boston, MA, USA

ISBN 978-3-030-03619-5   ISBN 978-3-030-03620-1   (eBook)
https://doi.org/10.1007/978-3-030-03620-1

Library of Congress Control Number: 2018962465

This Palgrave Macmillan imprint is published by the registered company Springer Nature Switzerland AG
The registered company address is: Gewerbestrasse 11, 6330 Cham, Switzerland

To Barry, William, Henry, and George

Preface

It was a cold day in Arkadelphia and we were shivering out in the muddy grounds of the sawmill. As part of my new role in Washington, I had gotten up at 4 AM, taken two planes to land in Little Rock, and driven two hours south to visit Richie and his wife Angela at their business, Shields Wood Products. I was not in a good mood. Then Angela, who was also the business's bookkeeper, turned to me and said the words that changed my whole perspective on the day and probably led to the writing of this book. "You know," she said, "you saved our business."

I heard these words dozens of times over the next year as we worked to get capital flowing to small businesses who were suffering because credit markets had frozen during the Great Recession of 2008. Banks that had become over-extended stopped lending, making loans guaranteed by the U.S. Small Business Administration (SBA) a lifeline for many. As the head of the SBA, I was the member of President Obama's Cabinet who was responsible for all of America's entrepreneurs and small business owners. It was a terrific job. But it sometimes required pounding the table to ensure the voice of small business did not get lost under the mass of other priorities.

I knew how important small business was to the economy. My Grandpa Jack had come to America from Russia at the turn of the last century with nothing. Starting with two machines in the back of a shoe shop in Boston, he built a textile business that not only provided for his family and extended family, but grew to employ hundreds of people. When I worked for him in the mill during my college years, he would tell me not to go to work for a big company. "Our family," he would say, "doesn't work for other businesses. We build our own."

Grandpa Jack's story was the story of the American Dream. Our country is one of the few places in the world where it is possible to lift oneself and one's family to a new set of opportunities and a new life by starting and growing a small business. This path to opportunity, however, is threatened. Access to capital for small businesses has been under pressure, not only during the recession, but for decades prior, due to consolidations in community banks and the difficulty banks have in making profits with small loans, particularly those given to the smallest businesses.

Beginning around 2010, however, fintech entrepreneurs have come on the scene. Using data and technology, they have brought a new experience to small business borrowers, massively improving a process that has essentially not changed since the time when Grandpa Jack sought a loan. Through their early success and some subsequent stumbles, these innovators are transforming the small business lending market. Large global banks and small community banks have woken up to the fact that small businesses are looking for a more responsive, more innovative set of products and services focused on their unique needs. Platforms like Amazon, Square, and PayPal are demonstrating the power of data to overcome the information opacity that has long made small businesses difficult to understand.

This book explores the current and potential future states of small business lending. It asks, "What do small businesses want? Who will be the winners and losers? And how should regulators respond?" But most of all, this is a book about the role of small business, its importance to the economy, and the prospects that technology brings to overcome some of the fundamental barriers to a better small business lending market. It seeks to define a new state— Small Business Utopia—a world of innovative solutions that will help small businesses get the capital and financial insights they need to grow and succeed.

At the center of this book is a basic premise that small businesses matter. They matter for economic growth, they are fundamental to our communities, and they are critical to the future of the American Dream. This has been my experience as a venture capitalist and a small business owner, and during my time in government. And it is confirmed by the stories of Richie and Angela, Grandpa Jack, and the owners and employees of so many of America's 30 million small businesses.

In October 2009, I was standing with President Obama in a warehouse in Landover, Maryland, filled with small business owners. The President finished his speech, looked into the faces of these entrepreneurs who were suffering in the aftermath of the financial crisis, and said:

I know that times are tough, and I can only imagine what many of you are going through, in terms of keeping things going in the midst of a very tough economic climate. But I guarantee you this: This administration is going to stand behind small businesses. You are our highest priority because we are confident that when you are succeeding, America succeeds.[1]

Small businesses are better off today in terms of access to capital than they were in the midst of the financial crisis, but obstacles remain. The rise of technology may serve to help small businesses overcome these challenges, forging transformative new products and services and a renewed pathway to the American Dream. In this period of change, we must ensure that innovations flourish in ways that enhance the prospects and prosperity of small businesses. Because, when small businesses succeed, America succeeds.

Boston, MA, USA   Karen G. Mills

Note

1. President Barack Obama, "Remarks at Metropolitan Archives, LLC" (speech, Landover, Maryland, October 21, 2009), Government Publishing Office, https://www.govinfo.gov/content/pkg/PPP-2009-book2/pdf/PPP-2009-book2-doc-pg1555.pdf.

Acknowledgments

A book is a long effort and is built from the input of many wise and generous colleagues. I thank Louis Caditz-Peck, Ronnie Chatterji, Diana Farrell, Bill Kerr, Barbara Lipman, Brayden McCarthy, Ramana Nanda, Richard Nieman, Robin Prager, Peter Renton, Scott Stern, and Jonathan Swain for taking the time to read drafts and give comments and edits that significantly improved the book. I am particularly grateful to Bill Kerr for his input and for the example of his book, *The Gift of Global Talent*, from which we took much guidance. No one contributed more to this book than Aaron Mukerjee, Justin Schardin, and Annie Dang, who researched, wrote, and edited with me for months, providing stories, drafts, and good judgment throughout. Many thanks to Jacey Taft for her efforts on obtaining the permissions for the stories and graphics, and for her daily support. Brayden McCarthy had the original idea to write about the gap in small business lending, after working at the SBA and in the White House, and was my coauthor on two Harvard Business School white papers that form the basis for Part I of the book.

This book had its origins in the time I spent in Washington running the SBA during the financial crisis. I want to thank the team at the SBA for their inspiration and dedication, particularly those in the field offices who spend every day getting capital into the hands of small business owners. The impact we made would never have been possible without the vision and hard work of the SBA leadership team, especially Jonathan Swain, Chief of Staff, who continues to work with me on these issues. Those that have worked in Washington know that nothing gets done without support from the White House and Congress. To this day, I am grateful to President Barack Obama and to Larry Summers, Gene Sperling, Valerie Jarrett, and Pete Rouse for their commitment to small businesses and to me. Senators Mary Landrieu and Olympia Snowe set an example of bipartisan leadership by working together to pass critical legislation that is still helping small business owners.

At Harvard Business School, the encouragement given by Dean Nitin Nohria, Jan Rivkin, and my colleagues in the Entrepreneurial Management unit was a critical factor in the decision to write this book, and the Division of Research and Faculty Development provided significant and much appreciated support. I thank Tula Weis, Ruth Noble, and the team at Palgrave Macmillan for the opportunity and for all their help. Glenn Kaplan and Rebecca Uberti provided design and wise counsel on the book cover.

The inspiration for this book comes from watching my family, particularly my parents Ellen and Melvin Gordon, and my grandparents, go to work each day in offices just off the factory floor and build businesses. I am grateful to them, and especially to Barry and our boys, William, Henry, and George, for their support and encouragement in this book and in all endeavors.

Contents

1

The Story of Small Business Lending

Half of the people who work in America own or work for a small business. They account for half of this country's jobs. There are more than 30 million small businesses in the United States today, underpinning our economy and the fabric of our society. These businesses operate in every corner of every state, and exist in every industry, from retail shops to oil and gas exploration. The story of the small business owner is often one of the community-minded citizen who supports the local Little League or the immigrant entrepreneur who builds a life of opportunity.

All of these small businesses are different, but they face a common challenge: it is often difficult for them to get access to the capital they need to operate and succeed. Until recently, lending to small businesses hadn't changed much over the past century. A small business owner would compile a stack of paperwork, go to their local banker, and often wait weeks for a response. If the answer was "no," they would go down the street to the next bank and try again.

While this might sound like a frustrating process, there are many who say that it is not a serious problem. They argue that many of the small businesses that have trouble accessing capital should not actually get it because they are not creditworthy, and that most small businesses don't want to grow, so have no need for external financing. They also argue that today's banks are fully meeting the needs of the creditworthy borrowers in the marketplace. These statements have some truth to them. Not every business who wants a loan should get one and many businesses don't want to grow. The lending environment is also much improved from the dark days of the Great Recession. However, these views are blind to market failures in small business lending, which have only worsened over recent decades.

© The Author(s) 2018
K. G. Mills, *Fintech, Small Business & the American Dream*,
https://doi.org/10.1007/978-3-030-03620-1_1

Small business lending is hard. In this book, we will meet small business owners—from Miami to Manhattan to Maine—who are struggling to get the right loan in the right amount at the right cost. We will meet lenders—from New England to Texas to Silicon Valley—who are trying to figure out which small businesses are creditworthy and how to lend to them profitably. These are not just isolated anecdotes, but rather, they represent the experiences of small business borrowers and lenders in a market filled with frictions. Using the best available research and data, we will show a picture of the gaps in access to capital for creditworthy small businesses, and the barriers that have made many traditional lenders less willing or able to meet their needs. And we will track how innovations in fintech have begun to address some of these problems.

Transforming Small Business Lending

Many industries, from music to telecommunications, have been transformed by technology, but small business banking has been slow to evolve. That is changing. Financial technology, or "fintech," is a broad category that includes innovation across the banking, insurance, and financial services sectors, as well as new activities in areas like cryptocurrencies and blockchain. This book uses a narrower fintech lens, focusing on the way technology will affect lending—specifically, small business lending.

Lending does not happen in isolation. Other fintech innovations, particularly in payments, will have a related impact as they evolve. But, for the purposes of this narrative, the innovations in lending, and in data and intelligence related to lending, provide a rich environment to explore the ways in which technology will bring changes to the market. The cycle of fintech innovation in small business lending is not yet complete, but it has ushered in promising changes.

Today, all that is visible are the "green shoots"—ideas that early fintech entrepreneurs brought to the market beginning around 2010, and the nascent activities of larger banks and technology companies. Based on analysis of the foundational elements of small business needs and current lending markets, this book describes the ways that technology can be truly transformative, opening up better prospects for both small businesses and the lenders who serve them. Such a positive future for small businesses may sound overly optimistic. But newly available and soon-to-be discovered ways that data and intelligence can change decision-making promise to alter even areas as "old school" as small business loans.

As technology opens the doors to vast troves of data, opportunities are emerging to create new insights on a small business's health and prospects. Insights from this data have the potential to resolve two defining issues that have faced lenders and borrowers in the sector: heterogeneity—the fact that all small businesses are different, making it difficult to extrapolate from one example to the next—and information opacity, the fact that it is hard to know what is really going on inside a small business.

From a lender's point of view, the smaller the business, the more difficult it is to know if the business is actually profitable and what its prospects might be. Many small business owners do not have a great sense of their cash flow, the sales they might make, when customers will pay, or what cash needs they could have based on the season or the new contract. Small businesses have low cash buffers and a miscalculation, a late payment, or even fast growth could cause a life-threatening cash crunch.

But what if technology had the power to make a small business owner significantly wiser about their cash flow, and a lender wiser as well? What if new loan products and services made it easier to create what one investor calls a "truth file"—a set of information that could quickly and accurately predict the creditworthiness of a small business, much like a consumer's personal credit score helps banks predict creditworthiness for personal loans, credit cards, and mortgages?[1] What if a small business owner had a dashboard of their business activities, including cash projections and insights on sales and cost trends that helped them weave an end-to-end picture of their business's financial health? What if this dashboard helped them understand all credit options they qualified for today and which actions they could take to improve their credit rating over time? And better yet, what if the dashboard, marshalling the predictive power of machine learning amassed from data on thousands of business owners in similar industries, could help a business owner head off perilous trends or dangers?

This future is appealing because it responds to the fundamental need of small business owners to be able to see and more clearly interpret the information that already exists, helping them navigate the uncertain world of their businesses on their own terms and plan accordingly. And it provides an opportunity for lenders to better understand the creditworthiness of their potential customers and lower lending costs as a result. We call this future state "Small Business Utopia."

It may be that this name overpromises the outcome. Small businesses are perhaps too varied to be predictable and entrepreneurs run their businesses with so much ingenuity and peculiarity that their insights cannot be replaced or even augmented by artificial intelligence. Small business owners have a reputation for being set in their ways, and might be resistant to technology. But they are also pragmatic. If new intelligence is developed that will help them succeed, they will find a way to adopt it. Small businesses are hungry for new solutions. They responded so positively to the early fintechs' quick turn-around times on loans and the ease of the online applications that they spurred traditional lenders to action.

In this book, we trace the progress of the fintech innovation cycle and explore what will be next and who will provide it. We build these predictions for the future on a fundamental foundation of elements we can understand today: the needs of small businesses as they access the capital they require, the challenges their current lenders face in meeting these needs, and the opportunities that technology is providing for new solutions.

Three Myths of Small Business Lending

In the course of this journey, this book takes on three commonly held misconceptions about small businesses and small business lending. There are often good reasons why countervailing narratives exist. Sometimes, they are partly true. Often, there is not enough data to know definitively what the actual situation is or to prove causality. This is often an issue with small business, as data sources are scarce. Fortunately, since the Great Recession, more research and analysis has been conducted on the importance of small business to the economy, the role of access to capital to small business, and the gaps that exist in the market. We take advantage of this new research as we explore three myths of small business lending.

The first myth is the view that small businesses aren't that important to the economy, and that most small businesses fail and probably shouldn't be financed. This narrative argues that the small businesses that succeed largely don't need external financing, and those that should get financing are already well served by the market. In contrast to this narrative, the early chapters of this book pull together the best evidence of the barriers which are preventing small businesses from getting the financing they need, and describe the underlying market gaps in small business lending.

The second myth is that traditional lenders were "dinosaurs" that fintech start-ups would soon replace. Subsequent events have shown that this initial expectation about fintech disruption was too simplistic. However, the potential remains for technology to revolutionize small business lending. The contribution of this book is to separate hype from reality—to pull apart where the disruption will occur and where it will have the most impact, both on the health and wellbeing of small businesses and their finances, and on small business lenders. Based on an understanding of the kinds of products that will best serve small businesses and their needs, this book predicts what will determine the winners in the future small business lending environment.

The third myth is that the primary culprit for the decline in small business lending is post-crisis financial services regulations, particularly the Dodd-Frank reforms.[2] Some argue or imply that if these regulations were reduced or eliminated, community banks would return to their former role as the critical providers of small business loans, particularly through relationship lending.

There is truth to the claim that small banks have suffered disproportionately from the burdens of post-crisis regulation and that changes must be made to ease the regulatory burdens, particularly on small banks. But deeper analysis shows that the morass of competing and overlapping regulation is not the only problem. Structural issues that have existed for decades are largely responsible for the decline in community banking. Innovation, particularly in the use of data, is creating changes that can improve the marketplace, but will bring new regulatory questions. The answer is not simply less regulation; rather, it is the right regulation that considers and anticipates the new challenges that a technology-enabled small business lending world will face.

Taking on these three arguments requires an ambitious journey, because it means delving into the data and evidence in three distinct areas of economic work. First is the macroeconomic and microeconomic debate over the importance and role of small business, and the gaps in small business lending. Second is the innovation literature, which helps us to understand how cycles of innovation work and what outcomes we can predict for the fintech revolution. Third is the policy and regulatory arena, which requires an understanding of both the current state of financial regulation and the debates over the future of regulation as it relates to data and artificial intelligence. The constant thread in this journey is the narrow lens of small businesses and their need for capital.

Small businesses are the key actors in our narrative, but not all small businesses are the same. To define which types we are talking about, we introduce a new categorization of the country's 30 million small businesses: sole proprietors with no employees, Main Street businesses, suppliers, and high growth start-ups. This book focuses on bank-dependent small businesses that fall mostly into the first three groups. We do not cover the capital needs of the relatively small number of high-growth firms that are backed by venture capital. They are vitally important, as they are the firms that could grow to be the next Google or Amazon, but they largely operate in a different market for equity capital.

There are a few other areas that are not covered. *Fintech, Small Business & the American Dream* is the story of U.S. small businesses and their available capital markets. The United Kingdom and China play a small role as examples of countries with different regulatory approaches, but the promising developments in global fintech, particularly in developing nations, is left for future exploration. Additionally, this book is about innovation activity in the lending markets and how technology might help these markets operate more efficiently. Government policy is covered in reference to the response to the Great Recession, and recommendations regarding the regulatory environment receive substantial attention. However, this effort does not suggest specific government interventions to further close market gaps or fully explore how technology might optimize government efforts to improve lending options to underserved segments, an area with much potential.

Book Overview

This book is organized into three parts. Part I begins with the problem: small businesses are important to the economy and access to capital is important to small businesses, but banks, which have been the traditional lenders to small businesses, face both cyclical and structural pressures. The result is a gap in access to credit, particularly for the smallest businesses who seek the smallest loans. Part II describes the rise of fintech innovations, and the new and old players who have stepped up to fill this gap. Although this fintech innovation cycle has moved in fits and starts, it has the potential to be truly transformative, for both small businesses and their lenders. Part III takes on regulation, discussing issues with the current state of regulatory oversight, and the principles on which a better future environment can be built. The book concludes with a look at eternal truths about small business lending and predictions for the future.

Part I—The Problem

Small businesses are the backbone of the U.S. economy. While most politicians and the public say they agree with this statement, small businesses are excluded from many economists' models and exert little influence in Washington policymaking circles. Yet small businesses contribute disproportionately to job creation and innovation. Moreover, the ability to start and own a small enterprise embodies the American Dream. Small businesses support a vibrant middle class and strong communities, providing a pathway for social mobility. Contrary to popular perception, not all small businesses are the same. This section describes four distinct small business segments, each of which has different needs, particularly with regard to access to capital.

Capital is the lifeblood of small businesses, who depend on credit to start, operate, and grow. Historically, small businesses relied on banks to access capital. But during the 2008 financial crisis, credit markets froze, and banks temporarily stopped lending even to businesses with good credit. This crisis hit small businesses hard and credit conditions have been slow to recover. The economic downturn significantly devalued collateral—especially home equity—that small business owners use to secure credit. Lenders and business owners became risk averse due to lost sales and the trauma from the crisis. Short-term cyclical factors made securing credit particularly hard for small businesses during the recovery, opening the door for the entry of new technologies and lenders.

After the recovery, there was still a gap in access to capital for small businesses. It is tempting to blame this on regulation or other cyclical issues, but longer-term structural factors had been putting pressure on banks for decades. Community banks, which traditionally devoted a disproportionate amount of their capital to small business lending, had been declining since the 1980s. The concentration of assets in large banks reduced the focus on small businesses. Larger banks tend to prioritize consumer banking, mortgages, and investments, often viewing small business loans as less profitable. Indeed, small business loans are riskier, have transaction costs that do not scale, and are difficult to securitize. These structural factors have reduced small business access to capital over several decades.

Against this background, we ask the crucial questions: what do small businesses want? Why do small businesses seek capital, what kind of capital do they need, and where are the market gaps? The majority of small businesses are looking for small-dollar loans, but the lending market is plagued with frictions that make it difficult for banks to deliver small loans efficiently. The gaps in the small business lending ecosystem and the capital challenges small businesses face set the scene for the potentially transformative role of fintech.

Part II—The New World of Fintech Innovation

In Part II, we explore how technology is changing the game in small business lending. Joseph Schumpeter, an influential twentieth-century economist, posited that innovation was the fuel that energized the economy through a process of "creative destruction." In his theory, new inventions would be applied in economically useful ways that disrupted traditional industries. Later scholars built the theory of the innovation S-curve, where new innovations live for some time in a stage of ferment, as markets become accustomed to new products and services, followed by a period of acceleration and market adoption. Fintech entrepreneurs, when first entering the market, appeared to have an opportunity to dramatically change the landscape of small business lending at the expense of banks. The process, however, proved more complicated.

The second phase of the innovation cycle, takeoff, did not occur as expected. The initial excitement around the entry of hundreds of new fintechs produced rapid growth and a loosely regulated environment that allowed for high prices and hidden fees, which caught some small business borrowers unawares. While the first fintech wave laid the foundation for greater changes later on, it soon became clear that the innovations brought by the new entrants were largely focused on the customer experience and could be replicated by traditional lenders more easily than initially anticipated. Banks and other existing lenders also had significant advantages over the newcomers, particularly in the form of large customer bases and low-cost pools of capital from deposits.

The aborted takeoff phase led to a second rich period of market development, which included the entry of a new set of platform players like Amazon, American Express, and Square. Their ability to use data foreshadowed a promising new world for small business owners. In this world, big data and artificial intelligence would be used to smooth out small business cash flows, enhance small businesses' understanding of their finances, and provide them with timely access to capital that fit their needs.

In Part II, we also develop a playbook for traditional lenders and banks to innovate in this ecosystem. Using Massachusetts-based Eastern Bank as an example, this section addresses the key question: how should banks and traditional lenders innovate in small business lending? We lay out strategic guidance for banks thinking about partnering with fintechs, innovating internally, or engaging with technology in other ways. This section also addresses the difficulties of bringing disruptive ideas and products into a traditional institution and proposes structures through which to overcome these obstacles.

Part III—The Role of Regulation

In Part III, we ask how the regulators should respond to existing and coming changes. The current U.S. regulatory system is inhibiting innovation and failing to protect small business borrowers from bad actors. While these problems have long existed, the emergence of fintech has made solving them more urgent. The fragmented "spaghetti soup" of regulators overseeing banking has meant that small business borrower protections have fallen through the cracks.

We propose new regulatory structures and principles for the future of small business lending, particularly in an era of big data and artificial intelligence—

drawing on lessons from the United Kingdom and China. A new regulatory framework should both protect small businesses and encourage innovation while recognizing that many of the new players will look different from traditional lenders. Collecting timely data on the small business loan market is a lynchpin of any new system, allowing regulators to identify market gaps and "bad actors." The optimal regulatory structure of the future will require bold actions to streamline the overlapping and sometimes contradictory jurisdictional issues. Regulators must also confront thorny questions that will be raised by the use of big data and artificial intelligence to deliver new products and services.

*   *   *

This book is the story of the transformation taking place in small business lending, and the impact these changes will have on the financial sector and the small business economy. In the future, the result will not be that all small businesses get loans, but there should be a better marketplace with fewer stresses, frictions, and gaps.

With the new entrants, there will be more lenders and more lending options. Improved data and intelligence will mean that lenders are able to identify and serve more creditworthy borrowers, and that small businesses will have more insights to manage their cash and operate their companies. The right regulation will enhance borrower protections for small businesses and create a more transparent environment. If this small business lending transformation occurs, the prospects will improve for small business owners to succeed and achieve the American Dream.

Part I

The Problem

2

Small Businesses Are Important to the Economy

In 2017, late night star John Oliver began a segment by noting something interesting about politicians and small business. First, he showed former Democratic presidential candidate Hillary Clinton saying, "Small business is the backbone of the American economy." Cut to former Republican vice-presidential candidate Sarah Palin making almost the same statement. Then a split screen of former presidents Barack Obama and George W. Bush intoning the same small business mantra in tandem. More screen mitosis followed until, in total, 34 politicians from across the political spectrum appeared, each touting the importance of small business in almost exactly the same words (Figure 2.1). In an increasingly partisan political arena, support for small business is a rare point of bipartisan agreement.

It's not just politicians who express support for small business—it's also the public. According to a 2018 Gallup survey, 67 percent of Americans have a "great deal" or "quite a lot" of confidence in small business—twice the average rate for all major institutions surveyed. Only 6 percent said they had "very little" confidence. Small business has consistently ranked near the top in public trust, second only to the military, and well ahead of media, government, religious and criminal justice institutions, and large businesses.[1]

Americans have great affection for small businesses and believe in their importance. But what exactly does it mean to say that "small business is the backbone of the American economy?" Are we referring to the importance of innovators and entrepreneurs who develop new ideas and start companies that grow rapidly to become the next tech giant? Or are we describing the Main Street shops and other small businesses that make up the fabric of our communities? How do we measure the impact of small businesses on economic

© The Author(s) 2018
K. G. Mills, *Fintech, Small Business & the American Dream*,
https://doi.org/10.1007/978-3-030-03620-1_2

Figure 2.1 **"Small Business is the Backbone of the Economy" from John Oliver's Last Week Tonight**
Source: "Corporate Consolidation: Last Week Tonight with John Oliver (HBO),"
September 24, 2017.[2]

growth and on the quality and quantity of employment? Since half of U.S. employment is in small businesses, we know they are important, but exactly how relevant are they, and why?

To understand how small businesses fit into both the economic growth and employment picture, we must clarify a point that often leads to confusion among policymakers and the public: not all small businesses are the same. High-growth tech businesses play a different role in the economy than the dry cleaner or restaurant on Main Street, yet each has an important place in helping America prosper. Supporting each type requires a different policy perspective, as each one has different needs, including for capital.

In this chapter, we draw up a new way to categorize small businesses and quantify the different types of firms that make up the small business sector. This construction helps us better understand the significance and role of America's small businesses, and sets the stage for exploring the markets where they access capital and evaluating how technology is changing those markets.

Is Small Business Important to the American Economy?

Surprisingly, economists have no analytical framework to understand the contribution of small businesses to the economy. Macroeconomists tend to focus on broad indicators, such as GDP, average wages, and the unemployment rate. In Keynesian models, consumption, investment, and government spending drive the economy. Since so much spending power lies with consumers and larger businesses, small businesses receive little attention from these economists. Monetary economists pay attention to inflation and what the Federal Reserve (Fed) does. In their assessments, small businesses are not relevant, as small business policy does not drive monetary flows or outcomes. That is the province of global markets, where small companies seldom participate.

When macroeconomists think about the contribution of entrepreneurs, it is often through the lens of innovation or productivity. As one economist observed, "No amount of savings and investment, no policy of macroeconomic fine-tuning, no set of tax and spending incentives can generate sustained economic growth unless it is accompanied by the countless large and small discoveries that are required to create more value from a fixed set of natural resources."[3] In this framing, the contribution of entrepreneurs who invest in and market new products and services should be captured as inputs to innovation and reflected as improvements to productivity.[4] But this contribution is difficult to measure. For example, it is hard to know how the advances that allow us to Google information instead of going to the library—or use Amazon instead of shopping at a brick-and-mortar store—translate into productivity measures. Arguably, surfing the Internet and binging Netflix have reduced productivity for many of us. Nonetheless, we know that entrepreneurs and the innovations they produce are important because they contribute to the "creative destruction" of the status quo that economist Joseph Schumpeter once argued was the price for a nation to keep or attain leadership in the global economy.[5]

Even with accurate productivity measures, this analysis of small businesses' contribution to the economy would be incomplete. There are only a relatively small number of high-growth small businesses, the ones we often think of as the influential innovators in the U.S. economy. Some economists have argued that these are the only ones that truly matter and should therefore constitute the majority, or even be the sole focus, of government policy. For example, Pugsley and Hurst write that policies that encourage risk-taking and support access to capital for all small businesses might be better aimed at a smaller set of businesses that expect to grow and innovate.[6] Others go one step further, arguing that "the focus of entrepreneurship policy should be squarely on spurring more technology-based start-ups."[7]

It is true that these high-growth innovative businesses contribute much to the economy. But try this thought experiment: imagine a world in which we fully subscribed to the belief that the other kinds of small businesses didn't matter much. If policymakers could identify the high-growth firms early on, they might reasonably decide not to waste time providing licenses to any other small businesses or support their efforts to start and grow. The economic argument would be that small businesses like the shops on Main Street were not worth government or market attention, as they fail at a high rate, are replaced by other businesses, and don't appear to add much to the economy.

In this imaginary world, small businesses and the loans and other services that support them would not exist. Without a small business lending market, there would be no private financing for small businesses, other than a few venture capital firms that focused on innovative, high-tech industries. The economy would be driven by large businesses. Every Main Street shop would be a chain restaurant or store. Except for a few high-growth entrepreneurs, sole proprietorships would not exist. The Uber driver would be an employee of Uber and the small-town lawyer would be an employee of a large law firm. The path of starting your own business and building generational wealth would be replaced by an entry-level job at a large company. A world without small businesses would dramatically alter the fabric of our communities. It would certainly change the way we lived and worked, and would affect the image and culture of America—and the American Dream.

When faced with the prospect of even an imaginary world without small businesses, the average American becomes upset. People inherently know the value of small business. A national survey found that 94 percent of consumers said "doing business with small businesses in their communities is important."[8] And despite the fact that many consumers shop at Starbucks and Walmart, the same survey found that increasing numbers of respondents expressed a willingness to go out of their way, and perhaps even pay more, to support their local small businesses.

When politicians say that "small businesses are the backbone of the economy," or when former NBA superstar Shaquille O'Neal stars in an ad for Small Business Saturday, they aren't focused on the high-growth firms.[9] They are talking about the corner grocery store or the mom and pop coffee shop. But, given their lack of importance in macroeconomic models, is the economic value of these small business just a myth?

Contributions of Small Business to the Economy

A deeper look shows us that the sentiment many attach to small businesses is reflected in economic reality. Small businesses do, in fact, matter to the economy. In contrast to macroeconomists, microeconomists see many ways that small businesses contribute to the larger economic picture. Their reasons fall into three major arguments: small businesses provide jobs, drive innovation, and act as a path to achieving the American Dream.

The most basic argument has to do with the size of the sector and how critical it is to employment and job creation. As Nobel Prize winning economist Robert Solow points out, jobs are the main way our economy has chosen to distribute wealth and other benefits.[10] Small businesses employ about half of all working Americans. As of 2017, 58 million jobs were accounted for by people who worked for themselves or for a company with fewer than 500 people.[11] In addition, small businesses created 66 percent of net new jobs from 2000 through 2017.[12]

The sheer number of employees in the small business sector warrants close attention from a U.S. policy perspective. If small businesses are under pressure and begin to cut jobs, the impact on national employment and wellbeing can be significant. This was the case during the Great Recession. From the first quarter of 2008 through the fourth quarter of 2009, small businesses shed 5.7 million jobs, 61 percent of the jobs lost during that time.[13] This sent leaders in Washington scrambling to figure out how to stem the damage. In the United Kingdom, the financial crisis elevated small business policy, particularly with respect to access to capital, to a central place in the government's agenda—an action that continues to have a positive impact on the United Kingdom's small business and fintech economies.

Some economists and political theorists argue that small businesses are important because they provide stability to the economy. This theory has traction in other nations that build their small and medium enterprise (SME) policies around promoting a robust small business segment that can grow and support a thriving and stable middle class.[14,15] Saudi Arabia, for example, began an SME fund in 2017 in an attempt to stabilize its economy and provide jobs to its growing middle class in the face of falling oil prices.[16]

Even among skeptics, there is widespread agreement that some small businesses play an important role in innovation. A subset of high-growth small businesses are led by innovative entrepreneurs who create competition for established firms and markets by developing new ideas that keep the economy from becoming stagnant.[17,18] These small businesses produce nearly 16 times as many patents per employee as larger firms.[19] In a review of related economic literature, Mirjam Van Praag and Peter Versloot concluded that entrepreneurs account for significant "employment creation, productivity growth and produce and commercialize high-quality innovations."[20] Entrepreneurship and the experimentation it engenders are important underpinnings of economic growth and success.[21]

Small businesses and entrepreneurship also provide a path for upward mobility. Research suggests that self-employment increases intergenerational mobility.[22] At the level of the local economy, studies found a positive link between small business lending through the U.S. Small Business Administration (SBA) and future per capita income growth in a local economy.[23]

Small business has long been a critical part of the American Dream for new Americans, who often start businesses soon after they arrive. Immigrants inject a greater share of economic dynamism than their numbers would suggest. According to recent research, immigrants make up just 17 percent of the U.S. college-educated workforce, but constitute around a quarter of its entrepreneurs, and account for a similar share of inventions.[24] A Kauffman Foundation index shows that, going back to 1996, immigrants have consistently punched above their weight when it comes to entrepreneurship.[25] From 1995 to 2005, immigrants founded a staggering 52 percent of new companies in Silicon Valley.[26]

Despite these attempts to quantify the impact of small businesses in the local and national economy, there is no clear framework that captures the contribution of all small businesses. This can lead to economic policy largely focused on taxes, research and development, and trade promotion, and geared primarily toward larger companies, leaving small businesses with the policy crumbs. Creating smart and powerful policy geared toward small businesses is a worthy objective, as it can have a positive impact on a large segment of our economy.

What Is a Small Business?

One key to economic insights when thinking about small businesses is to eliminate the confusion about the kind of small business being discussed. When we do, it becomes clear that each type of small business has a role, and each needs to be considered separately in terms of product needs and policy approaches. In response, we have segmented small businesses into four categories, quantifying the size and activity of each group. As the old saying goes, "What gets measured, gets done." But a corollary ought to be, "What gets categorized, gets measured accurately." The following categorization can help us measure, create policy, and assess the capital markets for the different types of America's small businesses.

The Four Types of Small Business

There is no generally agreed upon way of defining a small business. Most of us have a rough notion of what a small business looks like based on our own experiences. Economists, governments, bankers, and others each categorize small businesses by different measures: their number of employees, their annual revenues, or even the size of loans they take out. "What are you calling small?" is a frequent question.

Throughout this book, unless otherwise noted, we will rely on the definition used by the SBA, the U.S. Census Bureau, the U.S. Bureau of Labor Statistics, and the Federal Reserve, which all classify a small business as one with fewer than 500 employees. By that definition, there are 30 million small businesses in the United States, constituting more than 99 percent of all American companies.[27]

To illustrate the different types of small businesses, let's take a walk through a typical American town—Brunswick, Maine. Located near the coast, Brunswick's primary employers are the shipbuilder, Bath Iron Works (owned by General Dynamics), and Bowdoin College. New businesses have been opening in the industrial park, located at the former Brunswick Naval Air Station. One manufactures composite aircraft parts, and another makes health care equipment. These businesses supply goods and services to larger customers. Their employees are happy to get their lunch from the Big Top Deli, where Tony makes the best sandwiches at his shop on Maine Street (spelled with an "e" in Brunswick). Tony had the chance to open another shop in nearby Portland, but decided against expanding. Next door, however, the entrepreneur owners of Gelato Fiasco had bigger plans. With growth capital from investors and a local bank, they opened a wholesale plant and began selling Italian ice cream as far away as San Diego.

The aircraft parts supplier, Big Top Deli, and Gelato Fiasco are all small businesses, as are the fast-growing tech start-ups moving in down the coast in Portland. Although they are all small, they are different in many ways including the ways they require and access capital. Some need money to invest in equipment and buildings. Others like Tony are content with where they are, but may need a credit line to smooth out operating expenses. Each is an important component of the U.S. economy, but none alone paints the full picture of the small business ecosystem in America.

The 30 million U.S. small businesses fall into four main categories: non-employer sole proprietorships, Main Street firms, suppliers that primarily serve other businesses and organizations, and high-growth companies (Figure 2.2).

Non-Employer Firms

Most small businesses, around 24 million of the 30 million, are sole proprietorships without paid employees. These "non-employer" businesses include consultants and a range of independent contractors and freelancers, from ride-share drivers and painters to real estate agents and hair stylists. Around half of these businesses are full-time jobs for their owners, while others are side businesses.[28] Some people start such firms intending to eventually hire

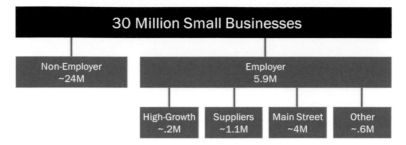

Figure 2.2   The Four Types of Small Businesses
Small Businesses by Number of Firms in the United States (Millions)
Source: Author's calculations using Economic Census data. This analysis is based on the work of Mercedes Delgado and Karen G. Mills, "A New Categorization of the U.S. Economy: The Role of Supply Chain Industries in Innovation and Economic Performance," MIT Sloan Research Paper, no. 5241-16, December 11, 2018.[29]

employees and expand, but many start them to accomplish other goals, such as having more flexibility over the hours they work. For many Americans looking to supplement their incomes, these businesses provide an attractive opportunity in addition to their traditional work.

Non-employer firms make up a growing share of U.S. businesses. Between 2007 and 2015, the number of non-employer businesses increased by more than 13 percent (Figure 2.3). Meanwhile, the percentage of American workers in similar types of non-traditional jobs went from 11 percent in 2005 to almost 16 percent by 2015.[30] Innovations, such as instantaneous global communication, have made it easier for people to work outside of a central office. Innovation has also promoted growth in the "gig economy," where people increasingly use online platforms to find independent contractor work as drivers at Uber or Lyft, as freelancers at Upwork or Handy, or even as dog walkers at Wag! or Rover.[31]

The growth in non-employer businesses has been driven in large part by people working full-time jobs with a part-time business on the side.[32] Whether this development is positive, negative, or neutral is debatable. On one hand, individuals now have more opportunities to earn money, and the hours of these part-time businesses tend to be more flexible. However, this may also indicate a structural issue in our economy, in that many people feel the need to take on an additional part-time business because their full-time employment does not pay enough. It could also be that many of these individuals would like to make their side business full-time, but do not have the resources, such as capital or skills, to grow the business.

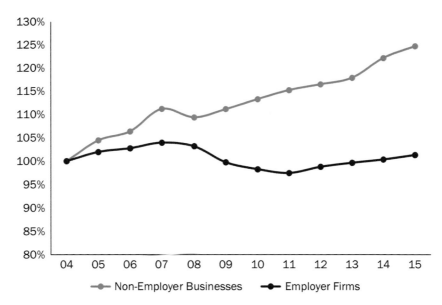

Figure 2.3   Non-Employer Businesses Have Grown Compared to Employer Firms
Growth Rates From 2004 to 2015, Indexed to 2004
Source: Author's calculations based on U.S. Census Bureau Business Dynamics Statistics and Non-Employer Statistics data.

Main Street Firms

The second largest category of small businesses is what we call Main Street firms. These are the local restaurants, gift shops, car repair operations, and other storefronts that come to mind when we imagine a small business. Most of these Main Street businesses, like florists and cafés, do not dramatically increase their employment from one year to the next, but together, these firms provide jobs and benefits for tens of millions of people.

Although the Internet is allowing some small firms to ship their goods across the country and around the world, Main Street businesses generally produce goods for local consumption. This contrasts with firms that engage in what we call the "traded" economy, in which businesses sell goods or services outside of their regions. However, the local and traded economies are linked through a "multiplier" effect. For every new traded job, two or more local jobs are created due to the demand of the employees at the traded firm to go out to dinner and use other local services.

Supply Chain Firms

A third category of small business is important but often overlooked: small firms that supply large firms and government clients. There are about one million of these supplier firms, which are often focused on growth and managed with greater sophistication than Main Street firms. An example is Transportation and Logistical Services (TLS) in Hoover, Alabama, just outside of Birmingham. Started in 2003, TLS employs about 10 people, has $6 million in annual sales, and provides trucking and logistical services to companies as large as Coca-Cola.

New research allows us to identify and separate supply chain industries from business-to-consumer ones for the first time. This work has shown how important small suppliers, which account for over 12 million jobs, are to the U.S. economy. Although most people just view suppliers as manufacturers of parts, the number of suppliers of traded services is growing rapidly and delivering innovation and high wages[33] (Figure 2.4).

Supplier firms play an important role in local economic growth and development. Cluster theory suggests that strong suppliers impact the ability of both large companies and start-ups to succeed. Co-location of companies and their suppliers leads to more economic growth and innovation, so a dynamic supply chain can be an important factor in encouraging businesses to move to or remain in the United States.[34, 35] For example, a research and supplier park established in Prince George, Virginia in 2010 contributed to Rolls-Royce's decision to locate some of its production there.[36]

	Supply Chain Traded	Supply Chain Traded Manufacturing	Supply Chain Traded Services
Small Firms (#)	1,152,173	160,623	991,550
Small Firm Employment (M)	12.3	3.6	8.7
Small Firm Wages	$61,856	$47,499	$67,865

Figure 2.4   Supply Chain Employment and Wages (2012)
Source: Author's calculations of 2012 Economic Census data. This analysis is based on the work of Mercedes Delgado and Karen G. Mills, "A New Categorization of the U.S. Economy: The Role of Supply Chain Industries in Innovation and Economic Performance," MIT Sloan Research Paper, no. 5241-16, December 11, 2018.

High-Growth Firms

The smallest category of the four kinds of small businesses, at least numerically, is high-growth firms. There are about 200,000 of these companies in the United States, but they contribute a disproportionate share of job creation. An MIT study showed that 5 percent of firms registered in Massachusetts delivered more than three-quarters of growth outcomes and had specific qualities that were evident even as early as the time of their original business registration.[37]

Most of the jobs at these high-growth small businesses are traded jobs, meaning where these firms are incubated or decide to locate greatly impacts the local economy. Cities have long recognized this and have provided incentives to attract these high-growth firms. As one economist argues, "Because a few, typically young firms grow rapidly and account for much of job creation, finding an effective way to support their growth is important."[38]

*   *   *

Each of these four kinds of small businesses plays a different role in our economy, and each has its own needs. A mom and pop Main Street shop has different financing needs than a tech start-up. The former might be best served by a bank loan, while the latter might need a patient angel or venture capital equity investor. A sole proprietor such as an Uber driver might need a loan to buy a car, while a supplier might need a short-term advance to hold them over until they are paid by the companies to which they are selling. It is not "one size fits all." The key to robust capital markets for small business and to effective government policy is to understand what it takes to meet the needs of each type of small business.

Fewer Small Businesses: The Long-Term Decline in Economic Dynamism

If there was ever a time to pay attention to small businesses, it is now. In a worrisome trend, the rate of small business creation has been declining for several decades. Researchers who identified this raised the concern that less firm creation would result in reduced economic "dynamism"—the fuel that keeps the American innovation engine pumping.[39]

For many years, economists and policymakers have understood that economic dynamism means new ideas replacing old ideas, and new and energetic companies and markets replacing incumbents. American entrepreneurship, and its ability to generate innovation, growth, and change, have been the envy of the world. A dynamic, healthy economy requires consistent firm creation,

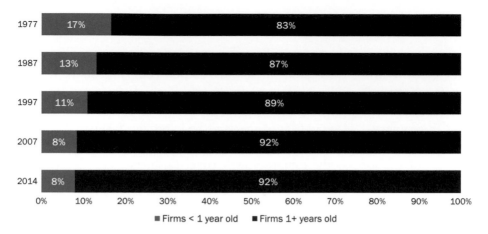

Figure 2.5   New Firms as a Share of Total Firms Declining Since 1977
Employer Firms: Firms <1 and Firms 1+ Years Old
Source: U.S. Census Bureau, Business Dynamics Statistics, Firm Characteristics Data Tables—Firm Age.

but between 1977 and 2014, the share of new firms in the U.S. economy declined by more than half (Figure 2.5).

As a result, job creation from this critical sector has slowed. Economic research has shown that new and young firms are the main drivers of job creation in the United States.[40, 41] But between 1994 and 2015, the number of new firms created annually dropped from more than 500,000 to about 400,000 and the number of jobs created by new firms declined as well (Figure 2.6).

America still has a strong reputation for innovation, perhaps best symbolized by the tech start-up culture of Silicon Valley. But recall that high-growth start-ups only make up a small fraction of all small businesses, and the number of non-employer sole proprietorships has been growing. A significant part of the decline in firm starts is most likely happening in the largest segment of employer firms: Main Street businesses.

There is no single, clear explanation for the long-term decline of small business formations in the United States.[42] Several economists believe that it may be a result of the simple math of having a smaller labor force.[43] As baby boomers retire, there are fewer working-age people, meaning there are fewer candidates to start small businesses. Another explanation may be the proliferation of "big box" stores, which can undercut pricing and offer a wider selection of products, and made it harder to start small businesses. The high cost of health care and increasing levels of student debt are also often cited as barriers to entrepreneurship.[44, 45] In addition to these issues, the market frictions dampening the ability of small businesses to access capital are much more pronounced for younger firms.

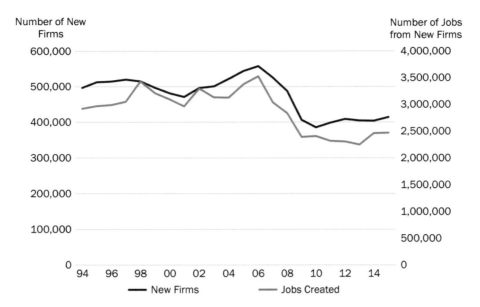

Figure 2.6   Decline in New Firms and New Firm Employment
Annual Number of New Firms and Jobs Created by New Firms <1 Year Old (1994–2015)
Source: U.S. Census Bureau, Business Dynamics Statistics, Firm Characteristics Tables—Firm Age.

*   *   *

The health of the U.S. economy depends on the small businesses that create the majority of net new jobs, drive innovation, and secure economic mobility for millions of Americans. In some ways, as technology puts pressure on repetitive jobs, small firms will be an increasingly important way to employ people displaced by large firms. In the next chapter, to address the issues that small businesses face, we explore one critical aspect of starting and growing a small business in America today: the ability to access capital.

3

Small Businesses and Their Banks: The Impact of the Great Recession

In 2015, Pilar Guzman Zavala was down to her last chance to seize the opportunity she and her husband had worked years to achieve.[1] She had to convince Jorge Rossell, the Chairman of TotalBank in Miami, to give her and her husband Juan a loan to open a new restaurant at Miami International Airport.

As she drove into the parking lot of the bank, she ran through her story one more time. Pilar would explain how she and Juan had rescued their business, Half Moon Empanadas, from the brink of failure during the Great Recession. She would show Rossell how they were now consistently exceeding sales targets, and how they had won the competitive bid to open a new location at Miami International Airport. The new location would be a godsend and was a perfect place for selling their delicious empanadas. Yet, despite their recent success at other locations and even with the airport contract in hand, they had been declined for loans everywhere they went, including at TotalBank. She hoped against all hope that this personal appeal to Rossell might make the difference. As she walked through the doors and up to the C-suite, she took a deep breath, reminding herself that no matter the outcome of this meeting, she and her family, and their business, were far better off than they had been just a few years ago.

The Zavalas were both immigrants to the United States—Pilar from Mexico and Juan from Argentina. Hoping to achieve the American Dream, they opened Half Moon Empanadas in a fashionable dining room in South Beach. The couple also had plans for a delivery business and ultimately wanted to create "a new category of food."[2] Pilar and Juan poured their savings into the idea and borrowed additional money through a bank loan to start the business.

© The Author(s) 2018
K. G. Mills, *Fintech, Small Business & the American Dream*,
https://doi.org/10.1007/978-3-030-03620-1_3

But soon after opening in South Beach, the Zavalas realized that they had misjudged the market for delivery, and they failed to hit their expected sales. They also had the bad luck of opening their restaurant just before the financial crisis cratered the Florida real estate market. As they struggled to find a workable sales model and weather the recession, they missed payments on a $350,000 bank line of credit. Attempting to make it good and gain financial flexibility, they used an injection of money from their family to make a $125,000 payment. Instead of stabilizing their financing, the bank responded to their show of good faith by cutting off the Zavalas' line of credit.

A few years later, having put $1 million into the business, including all their savings plus bank loans, they could no longer afford to pay rent. They were evicted twice from their business location and then, unthinkably, from their own home. Devastated, the Zavalas questioned whether they should continue with the business. They believed their concept could still work, because although the full-service restaurant had failed, when they took their empanadas to open-air markets and festivals, they could barely keep up with the demand.

Pilar and Juan didn't take a paycheck for nearly four years and avoided the temptation to declare bankruptcy. They adjusted their business plan, got out of their restaurant lease, and took over a food cart at the University of Miami. The previous occupants of the cart had struggled to make $100 per day, but the Zavalas averaged $1,500. Through trial and a fair amount of error, they found the kinds of locations where they could succeed. As Pilar said, "We dusted ourselves off, we tightened our belts, and we survived, never abandoning our bigger dream."

By 2015, when Pilar walked into Rossell's office to request an expansion loan, the Zavalas were operating three storefronts at the University of Miami and had the winning Miami airport bid in hand. Given their credit history since 2008, it was understandable that banks were hesitant to lend to them. In fact, they had only gotten the meeting with Rossell due to a timely introduction from Pilar's mentor. Fortunately for the Zavalas, Rossell looked past the numbers and saw that they really had turned things around. He decided to provide them with the financing for the new location. That bet paid off, with Half Moon increasing its revenues from $500,000 in 2014 to $3 million in 2017.

*   *   *

Many small business owners across the United States could tell similar stories to that of Pilar and Juan. Getting a small business loan is tough enough on a good day, but during and after the Great Recession, it became nearly impossible for many businesses to access the financing they needed. Even armed with a good idea, hard work, and a willingness to go to great lengths to fund their business, many small business owners were not as fortunate as the Zavalas. With bank credit frozen, small businesses lacking the additional cash to weather the storm were forced to close their doors. Those that stayed open often found themselves in the same position as Pilar and Juan—with rebounding sales, but an inability to access additional financing because the crisis damaged their credit and because of the long and uneven recovery of bank lending to small businesses.

The 2008 financial crisis was a wakeup call for Washington and governments around the world, as policymakers saw the effects of a lack of access to capital for small businesses. Although it was generally understood that access to capital was important to the small business economy, the United States had not seen such a shutdown in the bank credit markets since the Great Depression. In fact, from 2006 to 2007, credit markets for small business loans were so robust that the White House wondered if the government's role in guaranteeing small business loans was still necessary. The impact of the credit crisis on small businesses was unforeseen and devastating. In the first three months of 2009, the economy lost 1.8 million small business jobs, and more than 200,000 small businesses closed between 2008 and 2010.[3]

In Chapter 2, we saw that small business is important to the U.S. economy. But how important is access to capital to small businesses, and what happens when that access goes away? In this chapter, we will explore why the financial crisis was particularly devastating to small businesses to better understand the importance of a highly functioning small business lending market. The lesson of the recession is one we know from the work of economists: firms that depend more on credit suffer more from a financial crisis.[4] Small businesses depend largely on banks for their credit needs. When banks froze their lending, small businesses had nowhere to turn. Without the liquidity they required, many had to shut down their operations, adding to unemployment and deepening the crisis.

While the financial crisis of 2008 was sudden, the recovery in small business credit was slow and bumpy. Banks sustained severe damage to their balance sheets and were reluctant to take on risk. At the same time, the recession had dealt heavy blows to many small businesses' sales and profits. But the difficulties in the recovery were also an indication of a deeper problem. As we will discuss in Chapter 4, structural forces also resulted in permanent changes to the landscape of small business access to capital.

Why Focus on Access to Capital for Small Businesses?

Running a small business requires strong products or services, skilled workers, access to the right markets and customers, a trusted brand, and more. But underlying everything a business does is access to capital, both working capital for daily operations and capital to fund investments. While many owners of new businesses finance themselves or rely on friends and family to help, a significant number do not have those options or choose not to use them. In those cases, getting access to capital another way, most often through a bank loan, can be the difference between starting the business right away, putting it off, or not starting it at all.

Even once they begin operations, small firms tend to have more volatile sales and profits than larger businesses, as well as thinner margins for error. According to a recent study by the JPMorgan Chase Institute—which tracked daily cash flows for more than 600,000 businesses—the typical small company only holds enough cash in reserve to last 27 days.[5] The median cash buffer varies substantially across industries. For instance, the restaurant industry in which the Zavalas operate holds only a 16-day buffer period. This means that a poor month of sales or an unexpected expense can put a small business in a cash squeeze. Securing a line of credit for operational funding can smooth out volatility and provide a source of liquidity when cash is needed.

Access to capital is also important for expansion. When a sole proprietor decides to add their first employee, they might incur incorporation fees, have to purchase a payroll system, or need new office space. When a restaurant owner identifies a market opportunity and expands from one location to two, they will likely need new equipment, furnishings, and a point of service system. According to the 2017 Federal Reserve Small Business Credit Survey, nearly 60 percent of firms that sought financing in 2017 said they did so to expand or pursue a new opportunity.[6] These firms required a one-time investment that would often exceed what their businesses could generate internally, or what their owners' personal resources could handle. In these cases, they had to turn to outside sources of financing.

The Financial Crisis

For many years, little national attention was paid to the issue of small business access to capital. The U.S. economy, including small businesses, seemed to be doing well in the mid-2000s. Economic growth had been consistent, if not spectacular, for several years. Few financial policy experts, much less small

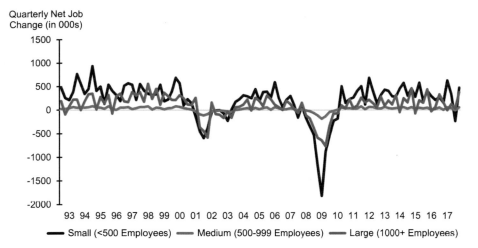

Figure 3.1   Small Firms were Hit Harder in Crisis, Representing Over 60 Percent of Job Losses
Net Job Gains or Job Losses by Firm Size ('000s of Jobs)
Source: Bureau of Labor Statistics, Business Employment Dynamics, Table E—Quarterly net change by firm size class, seasonally adjusted.

business owners, understood the risk building up in the financial system due to soaring home prices, exotic financial products, and highly leveraged investment banks. They certainly did not foresee that it would all come crashing down, sparking the most severe economic downturn since the Great Depression.

The Great Recession harmed the economy broadly, but small businesses were hit harder than most sectors. Between 2007 and 2012, small businesses employed 50 percent of the private sector workforce, but accounted for over 60 percent of the net job losses in the economy (Figure 3.1).

Small businesses were hurt more, in part, because they have fewer financing options than larger firms. Large companies can raise money by issuing and selling debt to investors in capital markets (and in the Great Recession, they could take on this debt at historically low interest rates). Larger firms have these options because they usually have longer, more established track records, less volatile incomes and profitability, and are considered less risky to lend to than smaller firms. In addition, they borrow in the larger amounts that debt markets have traditionally required. Small businesses depend on banks, and when banks are in trouble, as many were during the Great Recession, they tap (or slam) the brakes on lending.

During the financial crisis, banks and their regulators realized that the huge numbers of mortgages and financial products based on mortgages on their books were much riskier than previously thought. As the value of these assets dropped, banks didn't have the capital and reserves they thought they had.

To get back into regulatory compliance, some banks ended up allocating less money to small business lending. The four largest banks—Bank of America, Citigroup, JPMorgan Chase, and Wells Fargo—dramatically reduced lending to small businesses, relatively more than the rest of the sector. Loan originations for these top four banks fell to just 50 percent of pre-crisis levels and remained there through 2014.[7]

In addition, many community banks failed during the crisis. From 2007 through 2013, the number of U.S. banks declined by 800, including a 41 percent drop in the number of the smallest banks (those with less than $50 million in assets).[8] Since community banks are disproportionately large lenders to small businesses, this was an additional disruptive force preventing small businesses from accessing capital during the recession.[9]

Economic research demonstrates that credit markets act as "financial accelerators" that amplify both periods of growth and downturns for small businesses that rely on bank financing. One influential 1994 study showed that small firms contract significantly more than large firms when credit conditions are tight.[10] More recent research found that firms that are more dependent on banks for their financing suffer more during banking crises.[11] The Great Recession fit the pattern of previous financial crises in which the risk of unemployment was higher for people working in a sector that was more dependent on external financing. In effect, firms that couldn't secure enough capital from banks to fund their operations had to downsize.[12] Another analysis of the crisis found that, among all firms dependent on bank financing, small and medium-sized firms experienced the greatest drops in employment, partly due to the costs of switching lenders when their original lender ran into trouble.[13]

Government's Response to the Great Recession

By January 2009, it was clear that there was a crisis in small business lending. Lehman Brothers had failed, and banks were suddenly facing uncertain times. Some of the most important U.S. banks were calculating their balance sheets every few hours to see if they were bankrupt or could continue operating. Small business credit markets were frozen. New lending came to a standstill, and, even worse, many small businesses received a surprise phone call from their banker: their lines of credit had suddenly been cancelled—many times not due to anything those businesses had done wrong. Without access to liquidity from their credit lines, small business owners were forced to cut back on spending. This meant anything from delaying an expansion to missing a rent payment to laying off employees.

In the United States, the federal government knew that small businesses were in trouble, but the full extent of the problem was hard to quantify. In the West Wing of the White House, the economic team gathered in the early days of 2009 to discuss what should be done. The debate was fierce: should banks be forced to lend to small businesses? Should the government step in and lend directly? Were small businesses still creditworthy? What level of defaults should the government be willing to risk? The discussion was difficult because the exact data needed to define the state of the crisis did not exist. Despite bank regulation and quarterly call reports, there was no real-time collection of small business loan originations.[14] Anecdotes, however, were pouring into the White House and into congressional offices from small businesses like the Zavalas' who were caught in a credit squeeze and had nowhere to turn.

In the United Kingdom, George Osborne, the Chancellor of the Exchequer, noted that during the crisis, there was not a day that went by when he did not hear from small business constituencies about the depth of their plight.[15] As a result, the U.K. government made small business lending a priority, coming to the aid of their four major banks that together made up over 80 percent of small business lending. For the United States, the situation was more complicated. In 2008, the U.S. government took bold action, implementing the Troubled Asset Relief Program (TARP) to provide capital to banks and prevent their collapse. However, TARP legislation did not require that a certain amount of the capital infusion be used to lend to small businesses and keep their credit lines active. Although some banks used the capital for small business lending, most had what they viewed as more pressing needs. Between 2008 and the first quarter of 2012, outstanding small business loans (defined as the stock of commercial and industrial—C&I—loans under $1 million) dropped by 17 percent.[16]

In the face of the devastation, the United States had at least one often overlooked asset: a widespread loan guarantee network through the Small Business Administration (SBA). The SBA had relationships with 5,000 banks throughout the country and the ability to guarantee loans—a powerful tool that did not exist in the United Kingdom or many other countries. However, as the financial crisis peaked, even SBA-guaranteed lending had ground to a near halt, as banks pulled back and SBA securitization markets froze. In response, starting in early 2009, the SBA took aggressive steps to boost credit availability for small businesses.[17]

Before 2009, the SBA generally guaranteed 75 percent of the value of a loan. In early 2009, Congress passed the American Recovery and Reinvestment Act—popularly known as the stimulus bill—which temporarily raised the guarantee to 90 percent of the loan value, making these loans less risky for lenders to offer.[18] In addition, the bill eliminated almost all SBA fees. The combination worked. Using the new guarantees, more than 1,000 banks that had not made an SBA loan since 2007 made at least one during the next six months. The turnaround helped many businesses survive and contributed to three record years of SBA-backed lending from 2011 to 2013.[19]

More legislation followed. The Small Business Jobs Act of 2010 contained additional lending and tax support for small businesses. One program, the Small Business Lending Fund (SBLF), provided capital to community banks, with the stipulation that they increase small business lending. According to the U.S. Department of the Treasury (Treasury), the SBLF invested $4 billion in 281 community banks and 51 community development loan funds. Small business lending increased by almost $19 billion at those institutions from the time the program began.[20,21]

In August 2011, President Obama sat down with small businesses at Northeast Iowa Community College in Peosta, Iowa. One owner was visibly unhappy. His business had a government contract, but had not been paid for nearly a year. From that meeting, the QuickPay program was born. On September 14, the White House directed all government agencies to speed up federal payments to small business contractors from 30 to 15 days.[22] This acceleration of payment was designed to increase the cash liquidity of these small business suppliers and offset their need to seek credit in the still tight post-recession markets. The program worked. Payment times were cut in half and firms that received the quicker payments showed higher growth in employment, although the impact was less pronounced in tight labor markets.[23] (See box.)

Impact of QuickPay

Necole Parker is the Founder and CEO of The ELOCEN Group LLC, a construction and renovation project management firm located in Washington, employing 47 people. The company works with a number of federal agencies, including the Food and Drug Administration, the Bureau of Land Management, and the General Services Administration. Before QuickPay, Necole was constantly in touch with her contracting officers to make sure she got her invoices paid within 30 days. In addition, she had to frequently check to make sure she had enough in the bank to meet payroll. QuickPay's reduction of the payment cycle from net 30 to net 15 days allowed The ELOCEN Group to have a significant buffer of cash in the bank on a more regular basis. Necole reported that as a result of QuickPay and better cash balances, she was able to convince her bank to increase her line of credit from $250,000 to $1 million. In her words, QuickPay "had an incredible impact, [allowing] us to ... provide a better service not only to our clients, but to our subcontractors who help us with our capacity."[24]

The Slow Post-Recession Recovery for Small Business

Government action helped spur small business lending, but the recovery still took time.[25] Employment growth returned in 2010, but it took until mid-2014 for jobs to reach pre-crisis levels[26] (Figure 3.2).

Similarly, lending was slow to come back, as compared to past recessions (Figure 3.3). The levels of total loans in the economy, even eight years after the crisis, were below the recovery levels of any of the previous seven recessions.

The story of post-crisis bank lending was different for small and large businesses. The volume of C&I loans under $1 million dropped substantially during the Great Recession, and only reached its pre-crisis level in 2016. Larger loans, usually made to larger businesses, also dropped during the recession, but recovered more quickly and continue to grow at a rapid rate (Figure 3.4).

Why was the recovery so slow for small business lending? The financial crisis caused cyclical damage to both small businesses and small business lenders, which was deep and lasted well beyond the official end of the crisis.

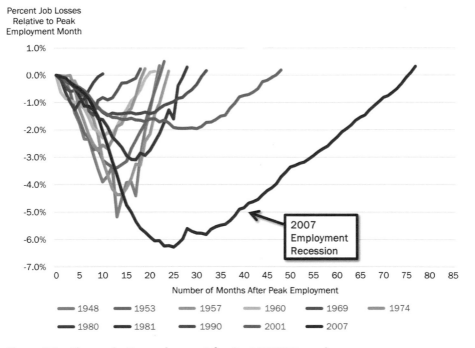

Figure 3.2   Change in Unemployment for Post-WWII Recessions
Source: "Current Employment Statistics," Bureau of Labor Statistics; US Business Cycle Expansions and Contractions," National Bureau of Economic Research; *Adapted from Bill McBride, "Update: 'Scariest jobs chart ever,'"* Calculated Risk Blog, *February 2, 2018.*

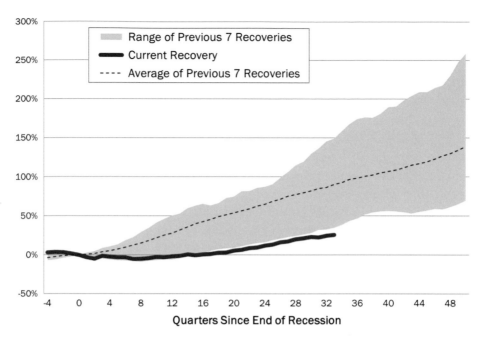

Figure 3.3   Growth in Bank Lending Since the End of the Recession
Source: "Financial Accounts of the United States," Federal Reserve; *Adapted from Steven T. Mnuchin and Craig S. Phillips, "A Financial System That Creates Economic Opportunities: Banks and Credit Unions,"* U.S. Department of the Treasury, *June 2017.*

As a result of this trauma, small businesses became less creditworthy and banks became more risk-averse, in ways that took years to reverse.

Cyclical Damage to Small Business Lending

One version of the narrative in the period after the financial crisis was that the market was functioning as it should: banks were not providing loans to small businesses because they weren't creditworthy. In the post-recession period, bankers believed that they were making loans to all viable small business owners.[27] At the same time, small business owners were telling stories of going from bank to bank and being rejected. The reality was likely a combination of a decrease in demand by recession-damaged small businesses and a slow recovery of supply by the banks.

Lending has always been simple at its core: banks make loans when they are reasonably confident they will be repaid. Banks ask themselves many questions when deciding whether to lend to a small business: does the firm have a good chance at sustained profitability? Is it managed well? Can it put up

Dec 2008 = 100

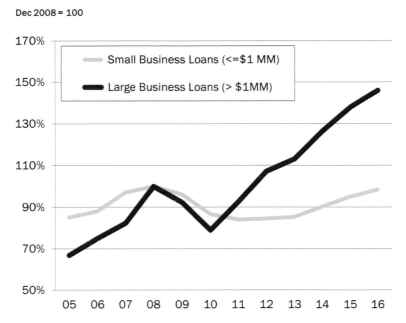

Figure 3.4   Comparison of Change in Small vs. Large Business Loans
Source: FDIC Quarterly Banking Profile Time Series Data; Adapted from Steven T. Mnuchin and Craig S. Phillips, "A Financial System That Creates Economic Opportunities: Banks and Credit Unions," U.S. Department of the Treasury, June 2017.

collateral to reduce the risk of making the loan? Can it find the workers it needs to start or expand? Do the owners have a track record of success and paying their debts on time? Is the economic outlook positive?

During the Great Recession, it became harder for banks to get to "yes" on these questions. The prime culprits were cyclical issues: declining revenues, damaged collateral for potential borrowers, and more risk-averse lenders facing new regulatory pressures.

Declining Revenues

During a recession, revenues can decline even for otherwise healthy companies. For about four years after August 2008, small businesses reported disappointing sales as their biggest problem.[28] The Wells Fargo/Gallup Small Business Index shows that, from 2004 to early 2008, 40 to 50 percent of small businesses reported increased revenue in the previous year. That metric plummeted to 21 percent following the crisis and did not return to above 40 percent until the second half of 2014.[29] These revenue issues had lasting effects.

Even when revenues improved during the recovery, the tough times that many small businesses went through in the recession made potential borrowers, like the Zavalas, look less attractive to banks.

Collateral Damage

If a bank can take possession of collateral assets when the borrower defaults on a loan, the loan is less risky to make. Home equity has traditionally played an important role in financing small businesses.[30] Unfortunately, the financial crisis wreaked havoc on this collateral, in large part because the crisis was built on an unsustainable bubble in the value of home prices. Once the bubble burst, home values dropped substantially, erasing trillions in asset value.

We do not know for sure how many small businesses finance themselves using their homes as collateral for a loan or a home equity line of credit (HELOC). In 2007, at the peak of U.S. home prices, the estimate was as high as 56 percent.[31] However, in 2011, after the collapse, a survey by the National Federation of Independent Business (NFIB) found that only 22 percent of small business employers either took equity from their homes and used it for their businesses or used their homes as collateral to finance their businesses. The collapse also left nearly a quarter of small business owners underwater on their home mortgages.[32]

Risk Aversion

In late 2007, with their balance sheets reeling and the devastating effects of risky loans like subprime mortgages fresh in their minds, banks began to tighten their credit standards. At the peak of the crisis in 2009, over 70 percent of senior loan officers surveyed by the Federal Reserve said that they were tightening their credit standards, including higher collateral requirements, calling in loans ahead of maturity, increasing the amount of equity businesses needed for new loans, and increasing personal credit thresholds. Credit standards remained tight until 2010, and only loosened slowly in the following years (Figure 3.5).

Regulatory Overhang

An excessive regulatory burden was at least in part to blame for the slow post-crisis recovery in small business lending. The Dodd-Frank Act required hundreds of new rules and regulations to be written, and U.S. regulatory

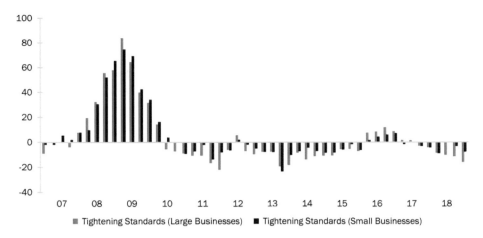

Figure 3.5   Tightening Credit Standards for Small Businesses
Quarterly Percentage of Bankers Reporting Net Tightening or Loosening of Loan Conditions
Source: "Net Tightening or Loosening of Financial Conditions for Small Businesses," Federal Reserve's Senior Loan Officer Survey.

agencies opted to develop others. One study found that regulation after the recession reduced the incentives for all banks to make very small loans, and also reduced the viability of banks with assets of less than $300 million.[33] Since Dodd-Frank, the small loan share at larger banks fell by nine percentage points, while the magnitude of the decline was twice as great at small banks.

A 2016 Bipartisan Policy Center paper found that while post-crisis reforms had generally made the financial system and consumers safer, they had also created unintended consequences. Some regulations were unnecessarily duplicative, or even in conflict with each other, causing firms to stop offering certain services.[34] Attempts have been made to quantify the costs of compliance to banks.[35] The American Action Forum estimated in 2016 that the Dodd-Frank Act had imposed more than $36 billion in final rule costs and 73 million hours of paperwork.[36] Estimates published in the Federal Register pegged the cost much lower, at $10.4 billion.[37] Other estimates of the total compliance cost to the industry vary widely.

What is clear is that increased regulation raised costs for banks, which made it costlier to lend and likely caused some financial firms to reduce or eliminate their lending to small firms. The regulatory burden seems to have fallen on smaller banks the hardest. In a 2013 paper, the Federal Reserve Bank of Minneapolis found that the smallest banks, those with assets of less than $50 million, suffered the greatest hit to their profitability from having to hire compliance staff.[38] This makes intuitive sense because the smallest banks have the fewest employees, so having to hire one more person for compliance costs relatively more than it does for a large bank that already has a robust compliance department. A 2016 paper from the Federal Reserve Bank of St. Louis presented evidence confirming that "compliance costs at banks with assets of less than $100 million represented more than 8 percent of noninterest expense, while the same costs at banks with assets of between $1 billion and $10 billion represented less than 3 percent of noninterest expense."[39]

An Improved Funding Environment

Despite these issues, credit markets eventually improved. The 2017 Federal Reserve Small Business Credit Survey showed that over 46 percent of respondents said they had received all of the funding they applied for, up from 40 percent of respondents in the previous year[40] (Figure 3.6).

It is important to note that this number should not be close to 100 percent. Some small businesses are not creditworthy enough to qualify for the full amount they request, and lending to them would likely result in poor outcomes both for the lender and the small business owner. However, we also do not want a market gap in which many creditworthy small business borrowers are being turned away.

Unfortunately, there is evidence that, despite the improved environment, a credit gap did continue. Even as late as 2017, small business loan assets held at U.S. banks had not reached pre-recession levels. In fact, by 2017, the share of small business loans as a percentage of all business loans at banks had dropped to about 20 percent, down from over 30 percent before the crisis (Figure 3.7).

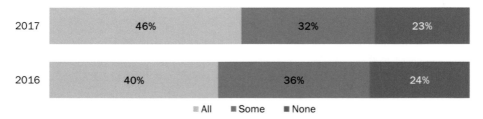

Figure 3.6   Small Business Funding Has Improved
Amount of financing approved (percentage of applicants)
Source: "2017 Small Business Credit Survey: Report on Employer Firms," Federal Reserve Banks, May 2018.
Note: Values may not total 100 percent due to rounding. Data from the 2014 and 2015 surveys is not included due to differences in sampling.

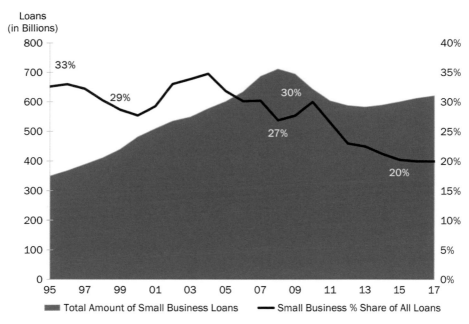

Figure 3.7   Small Business Loans at U.S. Banks, 1995–2017
Source: Author's analysis of FDIC Quarterly Banking Profile Time Series Data.
Note: Small business loans are defined as those under $1 million.

*   *   *

If the cyclical pressures had receded, then why was bank lending to small business still so low? Small business lending was also affected by structural changes, which had begun before the Great Recession, were exacerbated by the crisis, and continued in its aftermath. In the next chapters, we will explore these changes in the structure of the banking industry and the response of fintech entrepreneurs who identified the unmet needs of small business owners seeking capital. The crisis and the sluggish recovery opened the door to a technology-driven revolution in small business lending that may be changing the game for small business owners like the Zavalas. To understand the impact that technology and fintech innovation will have, we need to go back to the trajectory of the last 40 years of U.S. banking and explore the structural decline of community banks, on which small businesses have relied for their capital needs.

4

Structural Obstacles Slow Small Business Lending

In 2016, Rich Square, North Carolina—population a bit south of 1,000—found itself without a bank branch for the first time in more than 100 years.[1] Nearby Roxobel had lost its only branch in 2014, forcing small business owner Tommy Davis to drive 25 minutes each way to make deposits at his bank. Davis was not the only time-strapped small business owner facing this issue. These banks are the lifeblood of many local communities—rural and urban—and their small business ecosystems.

The financial crisis and the slow thawing of credit in the recovery that followed affected small businesses more than many others. But there were troubling signs for small business lending in the U.S. economy long before the crisis hit. The number of community banks, which have always been more likely to lend to small firms, had been declining since the 1980s. The Federal Reserve Bank of Cleveland summarized another problem: "The factors unleashed by the financial crisis and the Great Recession added to a longer-term trend. Banks have been shifting activity away from the small business credit market since the late 1990s, as they have consolidated and sought out more profitable sectors of the credit market."[2]

As we saw in Chapter 3, the increase in post-crisis regulation caused a disproportionate burden to small banks, which affected small businesses' access to capital. Some believe that if these regulations were reversed, small community banks would flourish again as they returned to their roles as the providers of smaller loans to local small businesses with whom they had relationships. But structural changes in the banking industry were also a root cause of the problem. Thus, the solutions are not as simple as just a rollback in regulations.

© The Author(s) 2018
K. G. Mills, *Fintech, Small Business & the American Dream*,
https://doi.org/10.1007/978-3-030-03620-1_4

43

Small Businesses Rely on Community Banks

Community banks are an important thread in our story because they provide a disproportionate share of loans to small businesses. In 2017, small business loan approval rates were 68 percent at small banks versus 56 percent at larger banks.[3] Given this, it is not surprising to find that, when compared with large banks, community banks dedicate a higher share of their assets to small business lending. In 2017, the smallest community banks held just 7 percent of the assets in the banking industry, but made 17 percent of the loans to businesses[4] (Figure 4.1).

What is it about community banks, their local presence, and the relationships they build that is so important in small business lending?[5]

Defining Community Banks

It's helpful to be explicit about what a community bank is. As with small businesses, there is no universally agreed-upon definition. The term most often refers to banks that are small—generally with less than $1 billion in assets, but sometimes going up to $10 billion—do business within a limited geographical area, and are focused on traditional lending and deposit-taking.

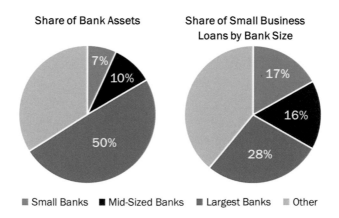

Figure 4.1   Community Banks Provide a Disproportionate Share of Small Business Loans
Source: Author's analysis of FDIC Statistics on Depository Institutions Report, 2nd Quarter 2018.
Note: Small banks are defined as those with $1 billion in assets or less, and mid-sized banks as those between $1 billion and $10 billion in assets. The largest banks are those with assets over $250 billion. Small business loans consist of commercial and industrial loans of $1 million or less.

These banks do not have the resources, geographic footprint, or diverse product offerings that larger banks often possess, but they tend to know the communities they serve more intimately.

To understand the advantage a community bank might have in making loans, imagine that Michelle owns an ice cream parlor and wants to open a second one across town. She runs into problems securing the financing she needs because three years ago, she was late on several loan payments, a red flag for lenders. However, a local banker who knows Michelle personally may understand that the reason for the late payments was a family medical emergency, that other locals vouch for Michelle's character and ability, and that her credit is otherwise spotless. That banker will likely consider Michelle a better credit risk than she would appear if her numbers were run through a standardized formula.

Small firms tend to be more "informationally opaque"—that is, they don't have as much publicly available, transparent information for lenders to review as larger companies would have. Local banks are more able to invest the time and personnel to build closer relationships with borrowers, which then makes it easier for them to assess a borrower's creditworthiness.[6] The economic literature indicates that larger banks are more likely to rely on standardized, quantitative criteria when deciding whether to make a loan to a small firm, while smaller banks are more likely to use qualitative criteria that look beyond the numbers to the applicants' personal qualities.[7,8]

Focusing on local markets and having more insights into the borrower may be an advantage for community banks. One study found that loans performed better when borrowers were located closer to their lenders. Borrowers 25 to 50 miles from the lending bank were 10.8 percent more likely to default on a loan, while those located 50 or more miles away were 22.1 percent more likely to default.[9]

Relationship lending can have additional benefits, including providing the function of monitoring loans and counseling small businesses after the loans have been made. About three-quarters of borrowers ask bankers or lenders for financing advice, making these sustained relationships valuable for the borrowers, who can run more successful businesses as a result, and for the lenders, who can provide more credit and other financial services to those businesses over time.[10] Research found that firms with longer-term banking relationships experienced stronger credit growth and lower interest rates during a financial crisis, and maintained greater investment and employment growth than firms that did not have such relationships.[11]

With higher approval rates and a focus on relationship banking, small businesses are more likely to hear a "yes" in response to their application at local

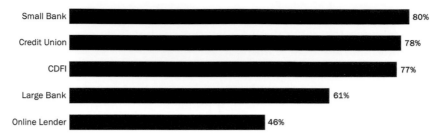

Figure 4.2   Borrower Satisfaction by Institution Type
Percentage of borrowers satisfied
Source: "2016 Small Business Credit Survey: Report on Employer Firms," Federal Reserve
Banks, *April 2017.*

banks than they are at larger banks. Thus, it is no surprise that community
banks are more highly rated when it comes to customer satisfaction. In 2016,
small banks had a satisfaction rate of 80 percent, similar to credit unions and
Community Development Financial Institutions (CDFIs). Meanwhile, satisfaction for large banks sat at just 61 percent and online lenders trailed the
pack at only 46 percent (Figure 4.2).

The Decline of Community Banks

Not every country has a large ecosystem of community banks serving small
businesses locally. In order to understand how this came about in America, we
need to go back 200 years to the early days of the Republic. Since the time of
our Founding Fathers, many Americans have been skeptical of an energetic
government and a powerful financial system, such as the one Alexander
Hamilton advocated, and have more or less sided with Thomas Jefferson, who
favored decentralized and relatively weak government. The history of U.S.
central banking is a microcosm of this ongoing conflict. Congress created two
central banks, in 1791 and 1816, only to see both charters expire under
Presidents Jefferson and Jackson. The creation of the third central bank, the
Federal Reserve, only happened after a difficult and acrimonious political
battle in the early 1900s.

   As a result, the U.S. banking system was often chaotic, with state-chartered
"wildcat" banks proliferating between 1816 and the Civil War, along with
more frequent banking crises than in many other Western countries. The
number of U.S. banks boomed with more than 10,000 commercial banks
operating by the mid-1890s. By 1921, there were more than 30,000 banks in
the country, an all-time high.[12] The vast majority were small and focused on
serving their local communities.

Number of
Community Banks
(in Thousands)

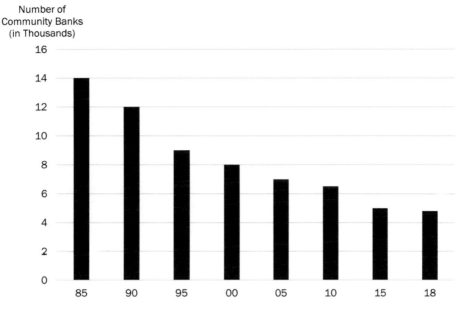

Figure 4.3   Banks are Declining, 1984–2018
Source: FRED Economic Data, Federal Reserve Bank of St. Louis.

After a series of failures in the 1920s and 1930s largely due to the agricultural depression of the 1920s and the Great Depression that followed, the number of U.S. banks dropped to about 15,000 and stayed roughly around that level until the 1980s. But midway through 2018, only about 4,800 commercial banks remained. Through failure, consolidation, and mergers, the number of U.S. banks had dwindled, even while the banking sector had grown much larger[13] (Figure 4.3).

The Banking System Has Been Growing More Concentrated

As the number of lenders was decreasing, assets in the U.S. banking system were becoming increasingly concentrated in a small number of larger banks. From 1984 to 2017, while the number of banks declined by 66 percent, the total assets in the industry grew from $3.7 trillion to $17.4 trillion.[14] Almost all of that growth went to non-community banks (Figure 4.4).

The largest banks have seen the lion's share of this growth. The assets of the four largest banks grew from $228 billion (6 percent of total banking assets) in 1984 to $6.1 trillion (44 percent of total banking assets) in 2011.[15] Another way to

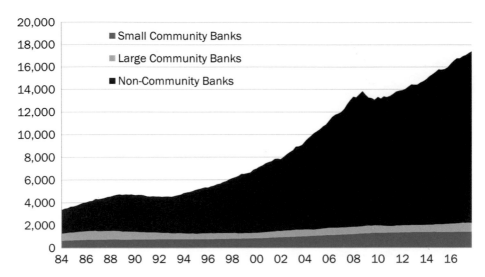

Figure 4.4 Total Assets by Type of Bank
Source: Adapted from FDIC community banking research project, "Community Banking by the Numbers," February 16, 2012.
Note: For the FDIC definition of large and small community banks, as well as non-community banks, see: https://www.fdic.gov/regulations/resources/cbi/report/cbsi-1.pdf.

express the widening gap between the smallest and largest banks is that, in 1984, the average non-community bank was 12 times as large as the average community bank. By 2011, the multiple had grown to 74 times as large.

The size of the average community bank also grew significantly during that time. Banks with assets less than $100 million accounted for essentially the entire decline in the number of bank charters from 1984 to 2011. Meanwhile, the number of community banks between $100 million and $1 billion in assets increased modestly during this period.

Wave of Consolidation

Until the early 1990s, most states limited or prohibited banks from acquiring or opening branches across state lines, while a few states even restricted branching within the state itself. These rules were put into place in the 1920s because policymakers worried that larger, multi-state financial firms would be too hard to supervise. As a result, the number of U.S. banks was kept artificially high.

After large numbers of small banks and thrifts failed during the 1970s and 1980s, Congress decided that the banking system was not concentrated enough.[16] They came to believe that small, local banks were too susceptible to local economic conditions, and consolidation would help them diversify their geographic risk. The Riegle-Neal Act of 1994 eliminated most of the restrictions on interstate branching and contributed to a wave of consolidations in the banking sector.

From 1995 to 1998, an average of 5.7 percent of banks consolidated each year. One analysis suggested that this was almost entirely due to mergers and acquisitions, which Riegle-Neal made easier.[17] The rate gradually declined, but between 2004 and 2007—prior to the financial crisis and in good economic times—3.7 percent of banks were still merging or consolidating every year. Financial crises also precipitated a decline in the number of community banks. Between 1984 and 2011, 2,555 banks and thrifts failed, mostly during the savings and loan crisis of the early 1990s, and during the 2008 crisis.[18]

Few New Bank Charters

Of course, bank failures and consolidations are nothing new. In the past, however, new banks would step in to fill some or all of the market gaps left when incumbent banks retreated. In recent years, that has not been the case. From 2000 to 2008, the Federal Deposit Insurance Corporation (FDIC) approved more than 1,000 de novo, or new bank, charter applications.[19] Before that, the fewest number of de novo charters approved in any single year was 15 in 1942.[20] In contrast, from 2009 to 2016, the FDIC approved a total of just five de novo applications[21] (Figure 4.5).

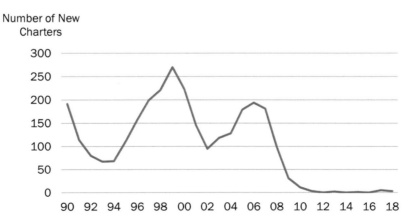

Figure 4.5   Rate of New Bank Formation Declines
Source: FDIC Statistics at a Glance, Historical Trends. Adapted from Kelsey Reichow, "Small-Business Lending Languishes as Community Banking Weakens," Dallas Fed Economic Letter 12, no. 3, February 2017.

One reason for the slow pace of applications and approvals is that the FDIC and other regulatory agencies have been more cautious since the crisis. *De novo* banks chartered between 2000 and 2008 were more financially fragile and failed at a higher rate than more established small banks.[22] After the 2008 crisis, regulators required a higher level of capital at banks to make them safer, and many would-be bankers saw the application process as too difficult and the level of regulation as too onerous. The FDIC has taken steps to make the process easier, and higher interest rates sparked a slight increase, but the number of applications for new banks remains historically low.

Impact of Low Interest Rates

It may be more than economies of scale that are weighing on the ability of small banks to compete. Former FDIC Chairman Martin Gruenberg is among those who have blamed long-term economic conditions for the dearth of new banks, saying that "low interest rates and narrow net interest margins have kept bank profitability ratios well below pre-crisis levels, making it relatively unattractive to start new banks."[23]

There is strong evidence for this point of view. The persistence of historically low interest rates has been challenging for banks, but especially for community banks, which rely more on loan interest income than larger banks. Net interest income as a percentage of community banks' assets has decreased since the early 1980s.[24] The advantage larger banks have over community banks in being able to efficiently generate revenue widened significantly between 1998 and 2011, mostly due to lower interest income.[25] In addition, low rates have limited a traditional advantage that community banks had of being able to pay higher interest rates to their depositors.

Consolidation Is Problematic for Small Business Lending

Bank consolidations and the disappearance of local community banks have been a problem for many small business owners. Tommy Davis, the North Carolina small business owner mentioned earlier, closed his Nationwide Insurance office in Colerain and moved to Windsor, a larger town 25 miles away, after the local community bank closed. For Tommy, it was "like a death sentence for a small town because the bank is the center of all activity."[26]

Economists have found that community bank closings have had a prolonged negative impact on the credit supply available to local small businesses.[27]

Interestingly, this decline persisted despite the opening of new banks. These results underscore the importance of lender-specific relationships and local information for small business lending. This information is often held within local bank branch personnel and lending systems, and can disappear or become less relevant if large banks bring in different personnel or more automated lending systems. Of particular concern are the findings showing that the negative effect on small business lending was concentrated in low-income and high-minority neighborhoods, where local relationships may be a more significant factor in lending decisions.[28]

Relationship Lending and Large Banks

As banks get larger, they typically have more branches, are more geographically dispersed than community banks, and have more employees to coordinate. Because of this, large banks need explicit rules and underwriting guidelines to keep loan officers rowing in the same direction and producing consistent outcomes.[29]

Larger banks, especially those with more than $10 billion in assets, are more likely to use a "cookie cutter" approach to lending, relying on standardized data such as a borrower's FICO (Fair Isaac Corporation) credit scores and financial statements. They find it hard to manage a relationship approach to lending and include "soft" or subjective information, such as a borrower's character, in their loan decisions.[30] In addition, larger banks tend to be less creative in developing customized loan structures tailored to a small business's needs. According to the 2017 FDIC Small Business Lending Survey, large banks use standardized small business loan products 65 percent of the time versus 9 percent at smaller banks.[31]

As the number of community banks declines and as larger banks create even more automated and standardized lending decisions and loans, the concern arises that there will be more market barriers and frictions. The smallest and newest businesses, especially those that do not have as much financial information or have endured financial issues in the past, will likely have a harder time accessing capital from traditional sources. More borrowers will find themselves judged only by rigid formulas, unable to make a case for themselves to a banker with an open ear, increasing the possibility that creditworthy borrowers will slip through the cracks, opening up further gaps in small business lending markets.

A challenge for the future is how to continue to capture soft factors, but also increase automation and reduce costs. Relationship lending is expensive and its cost tends to affect the smallest loans most. One solution is to "harden" soft information by finding new data that brings additional insights to traditional automated lending formulas. We will explore these new data sources and insights in later chapters; however, it is unclear whether these processes can ever fully replace relationship lending.

Small Business Loans Are Less Profitable

Another serious structural issue is that small business loans are less profitable for banks than many other lines of business. The chief obstacles are difficulties and costs of the traditional methods of underwriting small business loans, and the lack of ways for banks to offload small loans from their balance sheets, as the secondary market for small business loans is not robust.

Information about small business borrowers is important because small business lending is riskier than large business lending. Small businesses are more sensitive to swings in the economy, have higher failure rates, and generally have fewer assets to use as collateral for loans.

But, as we have discussed, reliable information on small businesses is difficult to obtain because the operating performance, financials, and growth prospects of small businesses are hard to see and predict. There is little public information about the performance of most small businesses because they rarely issue publicly traded equity or debt securities. Many small businesses are run by inexperienced or busy owners who may lack detailed balance sheets, understate their tax returns, or keep inadequate income statements. This information opacity makes it more difficult for lenders to tell creditworthy and noncreditworthy borrowers apart.

Another factor working against small business lending is that the cost of loan underwriting does not scale with the size of the loan. In other words, it costs about as much for a bank to process a $100,000 loan as a $1 million loan. That means that smaller-dollar loans are less profitable for banks. As a result, banks are less likely to lend at lower dollar amounts.

One response for a bank is to move away from small business lending and focus on more profitable activities. Some banks have reduced or eliminated loans below a certain threshold, typically $100,000, and some will not lend to small businesses with annual revenues of less than $2 million. Often, the largest banks will refer businesses below a certain size to their small business credit card products, which are usually more expensive for borrowers.

Most Small Business Loans Cannot Be Easily Sold

One way for banks to reduce their risk exposure and increase the funds they have available to lend is to sell off some of their loan portfolio. They often do this by securitizing loans, which involves bundling loans they have made into a single security that can be sold on a secondary market. This is common with mortgage loans, which can be easily bundled because most of them are underwritten using standardized formats.

Until recent years, there has been essentially no secondary market for small business loans. Loans to small firms are not easy to standardize, since they vary in how they are documented and the terms given to companies in different markets. In addition, there is a general lack of data available on their performance. One exception is loans made through the Small Business Administration's (SBA's) 7(a) program, which are sold with a government guarantee. Historically, about 40 to 45 percent of SBA loans have been securitized.

Creating a secondary market for small business loans is not a new idea. In the 1990s, Congress considered creating a government agency similar to Fannie Mae and Freddie Mac to sponsor securitization transactions.[32] In 1994, Congress took a different approach by reducing barriers to securitizing small business loans, but those changes ultimately had little effect.[33]

If accurate data on small businesses' credit were standardized and widely available, the securitization of small business loans would also be more widespread, making capital more fluid and accessible, and benefiting small business lending overall. This may be on the horizon. One set of new fintechs called peer-to-peer lenders have emerged who match investors with borrowers, and as a result, the details of each loan are published online. These lenders allow banks to purchase individual or packaged small business loans after origination to hold on their balance sheets.

Even with full disclosure of the underlying loan details, many concerns have arisen about the heterogeneity of small business loans and the ability to accurately assess the risk in a packaged tranche or portfolio. These issues and others have meant that the new secondary markets have gotten off to a slow start. However, as metrics-driven lending develops, the ability to eventually identify and describe risk pools may improve the packaging and pricing of small business loans and allow them to trade more seamlessly.

Searching for Small Business Financing Is Costly and Frustrating

As a result of these structural factors, even qualified small business borrowers can struggle to find willing lenders. Successful applicants for bank loans report waiting a week or more for the funds to be approved and transferred into their accounts. Research from the Federal Reserve Bank of New York found that in 2013, the average small business borrower spent more than 25 hours on paperwork for bank loans and approached multiple banks during the application process.[34] Some banks have even refused to lend to businesses within specific industries that they consider particularly risky, such as restaurants.

The reduction in the number and role of community banks has made searching for and securing a bank loan even more time-consuming and costly. Meanwhile, the low relative profitability of small business lending combined with a lack of accurate data on small business borrowers has meant that other banks have not stepped in to fill the role traditionally played by local lenders. In this environment, everyone is frustrated. Small businesses often feel that banks don't know them anymore and don't care about their business. Bankers rail against the post-crisis regulatory regimes and feel oppressed by the costly and confusing morass of compliance requirements.

The solution is to look forward rather than backward. The structural changes in U.S. banking are not likely to reverse themselves, even if the regulatory environment is optimized (Chapters 10 and 11 take on the flaws in the current regulatory environment and propose principles for a "smarter" regulatory structure). We will not return to an environment of 15,000 banks, most of which are owned and operated in local communities, anytime soon.

But there are other ways to solve the problem. We know that small businesses need access to capital to grow and operate their businesses, and that banks are increasingly finding these loans less appealing to make. But just because banks have not been making these loans does not mean that there are no profitable loans to be made. Chapters 6 and 7 focus on how technology is changing the dynamics of lending. Fintech entrepreneurs have identified innovative solutions to some of these structural barriers that have been putting pressure on small business credit markets.

But first, it's important to ask, what exactly is the problem we are trying to solve? The next chapter examines what small businesses want, including what size and type of loans they need, and identifies gaps where the current lending market is failing to deliver.

5

What Small Businesses Want

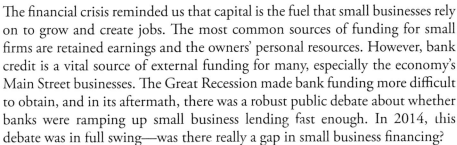

The financial crisis reminded us that capital is the fuel that small businesses rely on to grow and create jobs. The most common sources of funding for small firms are retained earnings and the owners' personal resources. However, bank credit is a vital source of external funding for many, especially the economy's Main Street businesses. The Great Recession made bank funding more difficult to obtain, and in its aftermath, there was a robust public debate about whether banks were ramping up small business lending fast enough. In 2014, this debate was in full swing—was there really a gap in small business financing?

The question was not an easy one to answer because of the lack of good data on U.S. small business lending. No one tracks loan originations to small businesses in the aggregate, much less in detail. Banks, of course, have the raw data about their own loan businesses, but it is not collected as part of the Federal Deposit Insurance Corporation (FDIC) call reports or other regulatory activity. The FDIC does collect data on the stock of loans on the balance sheets of banks, but since that number is a net of the additions and pay downs of loans, the flow of new loans can be obscured. Survey results, particularly from the Federal Reserve (Fed), are helpful resources, as are loan numbers from the Small Business Administration (SBA) and from reporting required under the Community Reinvestment Act (CRA). However, these sources of data don't tell the whole story.

Good policy requires real-time information on loan originations to small businesses. Other countries, such as the United Kingdom, have taken on this data collection successfully, viewing it as vital to small business policy. One provision of the Dodd-Frank Act (Section 1071) required the collection of this data, and delegated that responsibility to the Consumer Financial Protection Bureau (CFPB). However, the provision has yet to be implemented.

© The Author(s) 2018
K. G. Mills, *Fintech, Small Business & the American Dream*,
https://doi.org/10.1007/978-3-030-03620-1_5

Using the best available data, however, a worrisome picture emerges. In the slow recovery years, there was a gap in small business lending in smaller size loans. Banks generally define small loans as those under $250,000, but the most severe gap was for loans under $100,000.[1] For loans above those thresholds, and even more so above $1 million, there was robust competition. Regional banks such as Zions, Regions, and Key Bank had targeted loans between $500,000 and $5 million to fuel their growth. They saw that it would be profitable to give larger small business loans to well-run small businesses recovering from the recession or looking to buy equipment or fuel expansion. For loans of this size, the traditional model worked, with bankers cultivating a relationship and providing advice and additional banking services.

But what about the creditworthy Main Street business who wanted a small line of credit, or $20,000 to buy a van? Banks pushed these customers toward business credit cards or declined to serve them at all. This was a serious concern because small-dollar loans were what most small businesses wanted. Thus, for many years during the recovery, the smallest firms were having more trouble obtaining bank funding, in part because they were the ones seeking the smallest loans. This unmet need made the industry ripe for disruption by the new fintechs, as we will see in Chapter 6.

The Small-Dollar Loan Gap

How many small businesses seek outside financing and how many want small loans? The limited data sources we have tell different stories.[2] A report from Javelin research in 2016 showed that just about one-eighth of small businesses planned to apply for a loan the following year.[3] Meanwhile, the Fed's 2017 Small Business Credit Survey indicated that 40 percent of small businesses applied for credit in the past 12 months.[4]

We do have better data, however, on the size of loans small businesses want. Three-quarters of small business loan applications from employer firms were for small-dollar loans—loans under $250,000—and more than half of the loan applications were for amounts under $100,000 (Figure 5.1).

This means that 75 percent of the small business owners approaching a bank for a loan want a product that the bank would, in many cases, prefer not to provide or cannot provide profitably. As we saw earlier, it takes as much time and effort, if not more, to make a small loan as it does to make a large one. The revenue from the fees and interest are lower and the risk is often higher. Banks do make money providing credit cards for these small-dollar needs, as the fees tend to be higher and the credit process is automated. But

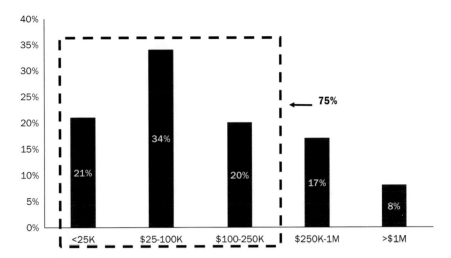

Figure 5.1   Small Businesses Want Small-Dollar Loans
Percentage of applications from small businesses by loan size
Source: "2017 Small Business Credit Survey: Report on Employer Firms," Federal Reserve Banks, *May 2018.*

credit cards are usually more expensive to the small business owner than loans, and not all expenses can be paid using a card, making them a less than optimal solution in many cases.

The Smallest Businesses Struggle the Most

Access to capital is the most difficult for the smallest businesses. In 2015, loan approval rates for micro-firms—those with less than $100,000 in annual revenue—were the lowest of any cohort of businesses. Micro-firms applying for loans faced a funding shortfall about two-thirds of the time, while companies with over $10 million in annual revenue had a shortfall less than one-third of the time (Figure 5.2).

It is unsurprising that micro-firms have more trouble with financing because, in general, the smaller the firm, the riskier it is, the more likely it is to fail, and the fewer assets it has to offer as collateral for a loan. The smallest firms are also the most informationally opaque. They often don't have complete financial statements and their taxes can understate their profits. Gathering a bank package to apply for a loan can be a long and tortuous process. And once it is completed, it is often not as compelling as it could be—the business owner may well be good at their business, but inexperienced in financial analysis and presentation.

Figure 5.2   Micro-Firms Have the Greatest Unmet Need
Percentage of loan applicants receiving full funding versus those funded partially or not at all
Source: "2015 Small Business Credit Survey: Report on Employer Firms," Federal Reserve Banks, *March 2016.*

Even controlling for credit score, Fed data shows that smaller businesses have a harder time getting loans. In 2016, firms in the "low credit risk" category with revenues of less than $1 million had an approval rate 10 percent lower than low credit risk firms with more than $1 million in revenue. In the "high credit risk" category, the approval rate was 20 percent lower for small firms.[5]

With this knowledge we return to the question: How important is the gap in access to capital for small-dollar loans for the smallest firms? Significantly, 80 percent of firms with annual revenues under $250,000 want a loan of less than $100,000.[6] Thus, this large pool of very small businesses—the same ones that are more informationally opaque and often riskier—wants the smallest, least appealing loans for banks to provide.

Start-Ups Versus Ongoing Businesses

Access to capital is also an issue for younger, less established firms. In 2016, about half the firms less than two years old (considered "start-ups" by the Fed survey) applied for outside financing, compared to 42 percent of firms more than five years old.[7] These start-up businesses had a more difficult time getting loans. Fifty-eight percent reported facing issues with credit access in 2016 compared to just 39 percent of firms over five years old. While almost half of the firms more than five years of age received all of the financing for which they applied, this was true for only about one-third of the firms less than five years old (Figure 5.3).

Banks rely on the creditworthiness of small business owners themselves in their lending decisions, which is even more of an issue for start-ups. According to the Fed survey, 92 percent of small firms less than two years old rely on the credit score of the owner to acquire outside financing, compared to 84 percent of firms more than five years old. These frictions in small-dollar lending and

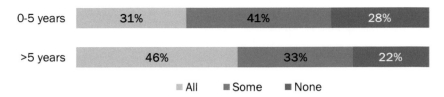

Figure 5.3   Total Financing Received by Age of Firm
Percentage of applicants
Source: "2016 Small Business Credit Survey: Report on Startup Firms," Federal Reserve
Banks, *August 2017.*

lending to new businesses were likely a contributing factor to pressures on
start-ups after the Great Recession—a matter that continues to be of significant concern for job creation and the dynamism of the U.S. economy.

Why Small Businesses Seek Financing

We have analyzed the supply forces at work in the small business lending
market, but what about the demand side? What do small businesses want,
why are they seeking financing, and what kinds of products will meet their
needs? Recall that there are four main types of small businesses and that,
for example, Main Street firms have different growth objectives than new
tech start-ups. Even inside a category, small business needs can differ. In
Chapter 2, we introduced you to Gelato Fiasco, an ice cream shop with big
expansion plans, and Tony from the next door Big Top Deli, who was satisfied with his single location. As a result, their business plans would require
different types of capital, in different amounts, with different durations,
and for different purposes.

One might think that the most common reason to take out a small business
loan would be to start a business. Because of lenders' resistance, new entrepreneurs who get loans rely heavily on leveraging personal assets by taking out
home equity loans or lines of credit. Even more often, they draw down savings, take on credit card debt, or ask for money from friends and family.[8] Over
two-thirds of businesses less than two years old were started using funds from
one or more personal sources.[9] Venture capital is important for a certain segment of start-ups with high-growth potential that need larger sums of money
and high-risk investors, but it is barely on the radar of most other types of new
firms as a source of funding.

As we discussed earlier, in this book we focus on small businesses that are seeking loans, rather than equity capital. We are looking primarily at the needs of the
Main Street firms, suppliers, and sole proprietors. Among these businesses seeking

loans, the most common reason is to expand—whether to open a new location, hire more people at an existing location, or perhaps buy a new machine to expand production (Figure 5.4).

The second most common reason small businesses seek loans is for operating expenses. Recall that small businesses have bumpy cash flows and often do not have a clear picture of their future cash needs. They also have cash buffers of, on average, less than one month. Therefore, many small businesses rely on a loan or line of credit to weather the uneven monthly or seasonal fluctuations. Linda Pagan, the owner of a successful millinery shop in Manhattan, found the slow periods in her business dramatically challenging, calling them the "trifecta of terror."[10] (See box). Linda and her hat shop are not alone in facing the anxiety associated with cash fluctuations. The small business owner's need for liquidity and capital to survive rough patches is fertile ground for the game-changing breakthroughs that technology can provide. In Chapter 8, we will explore some of these possibilities.

Small Village Shop in the Big City

Linda Pagan has owned The Hat Shop in New York City for almost 24 years. Based in SoHo in lower Manhattan, she provides specialty made-to-order hats for grand occasions, and for the everyday purpose of keeping the head warm in winter and protected from the sun in the summer. Linda believes in using local suppliers, usually other small businesses. Her feather provider is based in Queens, the fourth-generation company that makes her hats' ribbons and silk flowers is on 37th Street, and a basement studio on Grand Street blocks the hats.

Linda is a champion of the small businesses in her community. In 2009, the influx of large stores in SoHo spurred her to organize her block to form an association of independent business owners. In 2016, the area was designated the Sullivan-Thompson Historic District by the Greenwich Village Society of Historic Preservation, focused on maintaining the block's unique owner-operated small businesses and historic flavor.

But despite Linda's knack for building a loyal customer base and the high quality of her hats, she dreads the slow months, usually January through March, when cash flow can get tight. She dubs this slow period the "trifecta of terror." After Christmas, her shop experiences a seasonal drop in sales. At the same time, sales tax is due from the holiday season and by March, she has to buy inventory for the busy upcoming Kentucky Derby sales season.

2016 was a particularly rough year for Linda. Money was tight and sales were down. Instead of dipping into her savings, Linda took out a loan from an online lender, OnDeck. The process was simple: Linda provided OnDeck with her bank statements and business documents, and quickly received a $30,000 loan. She ended up having the best Kentucky Derby sales in shop history, and promptly paid back the loan with $2,000 in interest.

Use of Proceeds	Percent of Small Businesses
Expand Business/New Opportunity	59%
Operating Expenses	43%
Refinance	26%
Other	9%

Figure 5.4   Small Businesses Use Loans to Grow Their Businesses
Percentage of total small businesses surveyed
Source: "2017 Small Business Credit Survey: Report on Employer Firms," Federal Reserve
Banks, *May 2018.*
*Note: These percentages add up to more than 100 percent, as many small businesses
state more than one use for the loan proceeds.*

Customer-Product Fit—What Loan is Right?

More than simply getting access to capital, it is also important to make sure
that small businesses get financing that fits their needs. This means accessing
the right product at the right price and duration. This customer-product fit is
critical to a healthy small business credit market.

For example, short-term loans that are repaid in a few months work well for
seasonal businesses or for firms that need to purchase unusually large amounts
of inventory for holidays or certain times of the year. Longer, multi-year term
loans are a better fit to finance equipment or real estate purchases, since the
purchase is typically made to increase long-term revenue, which will then be
used to pay off the loan. If a short-term loan is used for an equipment purchase,
it may come due before the business has increased its revenues enough to be able
to pay it off. This could lead to a default on the loan, or a cycle of refinancing,
each time paying additional fees to do so. Ensuring that each small business gets
the right kind of loan is a win-win for both the borrower and the lender.

The main types of financing available to small businesses today fall into a
few distinct categories:

 Term loans are paid back on a set schedule. They are often used by
small firms to buy equipment or real estate.

 Bank lines of credit are liquidity available for a business to draw
down on an immediate basis to smooth out uneven cash flows.

Merchant cash advances (MCAs) let businesses—usually retailers who take debit and credit card payments—get a lump sum cash advance. The lender is repaid by taking a percentage of the businesses' future sales.

 Receivables financing allows a small business to sell or pledge some of its accounts receivables to a third party. In return, it gets immediate cash in an amount which represents a discount on the total receivable. This discount compensates the third party for taking on the risk that it may not be able to collect the full amount of the receivable.

 Business credit cards are often the most accessible forms of financing, but they carry high interest rates and are not permanent financing, making them less than ideal for ongoing working capital needs or for large, one-time purchases that will not immediately generate revenue.

 SBA loans are an option for some applicants who cannot get financing from lenders without credit support. In these cases, the SBA partially guarantees a loan made by an authorized lender. The guarantee makes the loan a less risky prospect, since there is less exposure for the bank if the borrower defaults. This incentivizes lenders to provide financing. Since women and minority-owned businesses have a harder time than others do when it comes to accessing credit, it is not surprising that the SBA over-indexes in these kinds of loans.[11]

How does a small business owner know what loan is right? In the past, the local banker who knew the small business owner helped make sure that there was customer-product fit. In the process of discussing the small business's plans and prospects, the banker saw the financials, assessed the use of the loan proceeds, and made a judgment as to whether the endeavor would be a success. This interaction allowed the banker to make an informed credit decision and the customer got advice and counsel about the right loan product.

As the presence of community bankers declines, who will take the responsibility for making sure there is customer-product fit? In a borrower-lender relationship, the interests of the parties should be aligned. It is not a good idea for a lender to give someone a loan that is so expensive that they can never pay it back, or one that has a timing mismatch. Maintaining optimal matching of the borrower to the loan that meets their needs is a challenge for the small business lending market of the future.

Filling the Gap

With a better sense of what small businesses want, we turn to the question of who will deliver it. As banks moved away from small-dollar loans and lending to small firms, entrepreneurs stepped in to fill at least some of the gap with creative solutions. Around 2010, new fintech entrants emerged in the small business lending segment, bringing a technology-driven approach to solving some of the market's issues.

The most visible initial innovation was a "digital first" approach where the process was done online, not in banks. The new lenders introduced a simpler credit application process and used algorithms to make quick and low-cost lending decisions. The new credit processes used more relevant and timely data from a small business's own bank account and other financial activities to make more nuanced decisions about whether to offer credit.

Most importantly, they created a better customer experience for the small business. Instead of Xeroxing a pile of paperwork, walking from bank to bank trying to get a loan, and waiting weeks for a response, small businesses could now apply online in minutes, have a response within minutes or hours, and have the money in their account within a day. These changes addressed some of the more painful frictions that had been plaguing the small business lending market.

The innovators were met with an early positive response from small businesses. The Fed's 2015 Small Business Credit Survey found that more than half of small businesses surveyed were dissatisfied with a difficult application process at their bank, while only one-fifth said the same about their online lender. Nearly half also expressed dissatisfaction with a long wait time for a credit decision from their bank, while again, only about one-fifth said the same about their online lender (Figure 5.5).

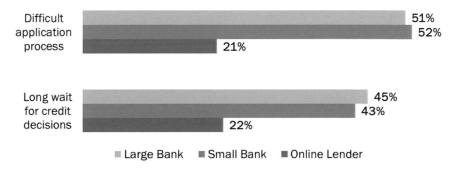

Figure 5.5   Borrower Dissatisfaction by Lender Type
Source: "2015 Small Business Credit Survey: Report on Employer Firms," Federal Reserve Banks, March 2016.

*   *   *

The stage was set for a cycle of innovation in small business lending. Finally, after much time and frustration, small firms and those seeking small-dollar loans thought that they would soon have many alternatives to easily access capital that met their needs. Using technology, innovators would fill the gaps in small business lending in ways that were good for the borrower and the economy as a whole.

Technology does have the power to solve some of the market frictions we have identified, and enable lending to more creditworthy borrowers at a lower cost and with a better customer experience. With the increased availability of data, lenders should be better able to identify the financial prospects of smaller companies, and because of automation of their systems, make small loans profitably. The resulting more efficient market should mean better matching of creditworthy small businesses with willing lenders, closing the small-dollar loan gap. Yet, as with many cycles of disruption, the story is not as simple as "they all lived happily ever after."

Part II of this book explores the cycle of fintech innovation that has begun to transform the small business lending market. After some early success, new fintech entrepreneurs faced powerful competition from large technology companies like Amazon, and banks and traditional lenders which refused to be counted out. For small businesses, the final outcomes are still evolving. Increased innovation has brought and will continue to deliver more products that meet their needs. In addition, artificial intelligence will enable new insights for both small business owners and their lenders, but will also bring risks as future markets operate under a regulatory system that has not caught up to the changes technology has brought. The next chapters explore what the small business lending environment of the future will look like, and who the winners and losers will be as the cycle evolves.

Part II

The New World of Fintech Innovation

6

The Fintech Innovation Cycle

In 1947, Bell Labs developed a small device known as the transistor. This miniature piece of hardware could control the flow of electricity, either amplifying or switching it. Using the transistor, electronic devices like radios and computers could be built more cheaply and reliably—and smaller—than their predecessors that relied on vacuum tubes. The transistor formed the basis for the electronics industry, perhaps the most economically and culturally important sector in the world. Most often built using silicon, the transistor created Silicon Valley in both substance and name.

But as important as the invention later became, it received little notice at first. Design and production problems had to be resolved. Potential had to be translated into concrete products. It was unclear how the innovation would go to market, and how large the market would be for it once it did. Ten years later, after a slow start, transistors had reached mainstream product markets and could be found in radios, hearing aids, clocks, phonographs, and more.[1]

In the late 1950s, another transformative event occurred. Jack Kilby at Texas Instruments patented the integrated circuit, which placed transistors and other components onto a single chip. Engineers worked to cram more and more transistors onto a chip, boosting their functionality along the way. This led to further innovations through miniaturization, plummeting costs, and ever more powerful chips that enabled the creation of personal computers in the 1970s, and eventually led to today's iPhones, Internet infrastructure, on-board automobile computers, and even pet tracking devices.

Today, we rely on a chip that can hold hundreds of millions of transistors every time we pick up our smartphones or our computers. What began as a

© The Author(s) 2018
K. G. Mills, *Fintech, Small Business & the American Dream*,
https://doi.org/10.1007/978-3-030-03620-1_6

simple invention to direct electric currents eventually gave us the modern-day products and services that transform how we conduct many facets of our daily lives. Yet, in 1947 and in the early years after the initial discovery, the transformative nature of the transistor was unclear.

While we are not necessarily predicting that innovations in fintech will be as transformative as the transistor or integrated circuit, the change to online, data-driven lending is the start of a significant cycle of innovation in a market that has not, up until recently, seen much change. Fintech covers a broad array of new technologies, from blockchain to online mortgages, of which the changes in small business lending are just one part. The path of innovation in small business lending will be influenced by activity in other parts of financial services, including consumer lending, payments, and artificial intelligence. But it will ultimately follow its own distinct course.

We are at the beginning of the fintech innovation cycle. The early innovations we have seen in online lending are like the phase of the transistor, opening the door to a new future in the way that small businesses access capital. What will be the "chip" that unleashes the full potential of these changes?

The Innovation Life Cycle

The creation of the transistor and its integration into the now ubiquitous chip is an example of how the innovation cycle works in action. An invention or fundamental change occurs in a market, and is at first adopted by just a few "first movers." The use cases for the innovation are unclear and the players who go to market often take on substantial risk, with the potential for large market share if the innovation is commercially successful. As more entrepreneurs understand the innovation's potential and translate it into new products and industries, the innovation becomes more widespread. Eventually, products become standardized and the market reaches a large scale with strong acceptance and usage. Then, new innovations come into play that compete with the old products, and thus begins the next innovation cycle.

These innovation cycles create economic progress. Joseph Schumpeter, one of the most influential economists of the twentieth century, was known for his work on innovation and business cycle theory. Schumpeter did not see economic growth as a gradual, steady climb like many economists did. Instead, he believed growth came from innovation, which was, in his words, "more like a series of explosions" than a gentle, continual transformation.[2] These discontinuous innovations overturned old ways of doing things and destroyed incumbent firms, and even entire industries.

Schumpeter cast the entrepreneur as the hero of his economic story, leading what he described as a "process of industrial mutation ... that incessantly revolutionizes the economic structure from within, incessantly destroying the old one, incessantly creating a new one. This process of Creative Destruction is the essential fact about capitalism."[3] For Schumpeter, innovation was not invention *per se*, but rather the application of inventions in economically useful ways. Innovation could mean a new product, a new process of production, opening up a new market, securing a new source of supply for production, or designing a new market structure for an industry, such as by creating or breaking up a monopoly.[4]

Later in the twentieth century, several scholars built on Schumpeter's work, including Everett Rogers, who popularized the innovation S-curve in his 1962 book on the diffusion of innovations. Others have since adapted Rogers' S-curve to include a four-stage life cycle for innovations: Ferment, Takeoff, Maturity, and Discontinuity.[5] Ferment describes the early stages of an innovation when the products and uses are not fully understood, and new avenues are being explored. Takeoff is the growth phase in which new companies, new products, and new customers fuel a rapid increase in adoption and usage. Eventually, sometimes after many years, a market reaches the maturity phase. Finally, discontinuity occurs when the market is overtaken by another innovation.

Our story of the transistor was just one example of how innovation follows the S-curve pattern, but there are plenty of other cases as well. Think, for example, about videocassette recorders (VCRs). The forerunners of VCRs were massive and expensive magnetic tape recorders, first invented in the 1950s. It was not until the 1970s that the VCR format was standardized and made affordable enough for mass consumer adoption. By the 1980s, two major formats had shaped the market: JVC's VHS and Sony's Betamax. VHS won the format war largely because its cassettes allowed for longer recording times—a major selling point for consumers. By the late 1980s, the VCR was maturing, growing primarily from movie rentals and making VCR ownership widespread.[6] Finally, in 1995, DVDs were introduced, disrupting the market quickly due to the smaller size and superior capabilities of the disks.

Financial Services and the Innovation Life Cycle

In banking, the automated teller machine (ATM) was a visible example of the innovation cycle. First introduced in the late 1960s purely to dispense cash, it caught on in the 1970s as banks added functionality that allowed customers to conduct other banking services such as deposits. By 1980, shared networks proliferated and banks began to view ATMs as necessities, and finally, as replacements for branches. From the late 1990s to the present, ATMs have remained common, but new innovations have moved customers toward Internet and mobile banking, and debit cards have made cash less important for payment transactions.

The evolution of banking services reflects the changes that have occurred in payment technologies, beginning over four centuries ago. This evolution can be envisioned as a series of S-curves (Figure 6.1). In Europe, physical money and checks were gradually accepted as payment starting in the 1600s. They were disrupted by a series of innovations—credit and debit cards, electronic payments, and ATMs in the 1960s to 1980s—which caused the number of checks written to peak in 1995 and decline ever since. In more recent years, e-payments have begun giving way to online banking and mobile money, such as Venmo and ApplePay. Contemporary innovations such as cryptocurrencies and distributed ledger technology may fail to take hold, or they may represent the next innovation discontinuity in payments.

However, with the exception of changes in payments, the banking sector has generally been slower to adopt innovation than many other industries. When innovation has occurred, small business products have often been the

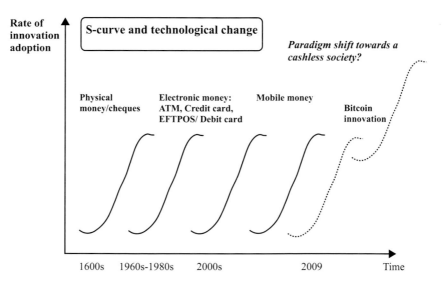

Figure 6.1   The Evolution of Payment Technologies
Source: Jarunee Wonglimpiyarat, "S-curve Trajectories of Electronic Money," The Journal of High Technology Management Research *27, no. 1 (2016).*

last ones affected. Until the small business fintech innovation cycle began in about 2010, small business lending was still a tedious process and decisions about whether to extend credit were generally made slowly, using personal underwriting and methods of assessment that had not changed in many decades. Small business lending was long overdue for innovation.

Why Did Innovation Lag in Small Business Lending?

With the advent of the Internet, entrepreneurs began challenging old-line industries in earnest. The technology to move lending completely online existed before 2005. Why had marketing, underwriting, and servicing of loans—particularly small business loans—largely taken a back seat?

There are several possible explanations for the slow pace of innovation in lending, and in small business lending in particular. First, the banking sector is heavily regulated. With so many industries and markets ripe for innovation in the age of the Internet, many entrepreneurs may have seen the financial sector, with its heavy overlay of rules, as an unappealing market. Second, the high level of regulation and supervision engendered a risk-avoidance culture at many banks. Banks employ armies of people whose job it is to ensure that they accurately assess and manage their risks. It can be difficult for an organization with a risk-averse culture to accomplish innovative internal change.

An example of the regulatory overhang on innovation in banking is the ability to deposit and handle checks electronically. Traditionally, banks were required to transfer original paper checks among themselves to make payments, and depositors received their paper checks in their monthly bank statements. In 2003, Congress passed a law known as Check 21, which allowed deposits to be made with electronic photos of checks, and for banks to transfer checks electronically as well.[7] Although the technology to do this existed well before, it required a new law to provide the convenience and cost reduction of electronic check deposits that we now expect.

A third barrier to innovation is the fact that the small business loan market is more heterogeneous than the consumer market. Mortgages, for example, are largely standardized and simple for the market to understand and securitize. Small business loans involve more risk in part because each business is different and their needs vary according to their industry, age, financial history, and other factors.

A final possibility is the relative size of the small business lending market. According to the Federal Deposit Insurance Corporation (FDIC), U.S. banks held $352 billion in Commercial and Industrial (C&I) loans of less than $1 million—a good proxy for the stock of small business loans.[8] In addition, there was $493 billion in spending on small business credit cards in 2017.[9] These numbers add up to just over $845 billion in small business credit, which is large in absolute terms, but small relative to the consumer market. Banks held about $1.7 trillion in consumer loans on their balance sheets in mid-2018.[10] In addition, the Federal Reserve Bank of St. Louis estimated the total consumer credit owned and securitized as more than twice as large, or about $3.9 trillion, plus another $2.2 trillion in residential real estate loans.[11,12]

Although small business lending was clearly an important segment for many banks, it was not the largest source of activity or profit, and not the priority for innovation. For JPMorgan Chase, although small business has been mentioned often in the CEO's speeches and in the company's annual report, the small business lending segment constituted just $22 billion out of a lending portfolio of $688 billion in 2017.[13] The voices of small business customers were not loud enough to demand more convenience and better service. Until faced with a real threat of disruption by fintech innovators, the traditional industry players felt little pressure to change the way they provided services to small businesses.

The Small Business Lending Innovation Curve

The first phase of innovation in small business lending emerged as the recovery from the 2008 credit crisis took hold. Fintech lenders had been around before then, most notably CAN Capital, which was founded in 1998 and pioneered the merchant cash advance (MCA).[14] But OnDeck really provided the first noteworthy small business focused innovative lending approach. Why not, asked OnDeck founder Mitch Jacobs, use the actual data from a business's bank account—including the record of what bills they had recently paid—to help determine their creditworthiness? This information was more current than the traditional measures used in small business credit, primarily the business owner's personal FICO (Fair Isaac Corporation) score. As Jacobs put it, "The time is right, the adoption of software by businesses is high, and there's an opportunity for businesses to quickly create a full data profile that minimizes risk for lenders and opens up a vast sum of capital for the small business owner."[15]

In the Great Recession, FICO scores had indeed proven unreliable predictors of default risk, and many like Bank of America, which had relied on them extensively in 2005 to 2007 to make automated loans, had withdrawn from the small business lending market with heavy losses.[16] And, as we discussed in Chapter 3, banks' slow return to small business lending in the aftermath of the recession, particularly to the less profitable small-dollar loan segment, left a gap in the market that innovators like Jacobs began to fill.

Ferment

The first, or ferment, phase of the online small business lending innovation cycle relied on available technology to rethink two longstanding frictions in the small business lending market: the speed and ease of the customer experience and the visibility of small business finances to lenders for credit underwriting. These pain points were not new, and the technology being used was not groundbreaking, but early fintechs such as OnDeck, Lending Club, and Kabbage gained momentum by creating experiences that were simpler and faster for small business customers. The applications were easy to complete, taking about half an hour at the time, and money could be in the business's bank account within days.

For small businesses, this time frame was unheard of, and for many it was the decision driver. Despite higher pricing, borrowers flocked to the new offerings, drawn by this superior and attractive customer experience. The first concrete analysis of the appeal of the new online products came in the 2015 Federal Reserve (Fed) Small Business Credit Survey. A shocking 20 percent of small business applicants reported applying for online loans, even more than were applying to credit unions (Figure 6.2). While the initial belief was that these respondents were applying to fintech companies, it later became clear that many were actually using their bank's online application, so the number applying to fintechs was likely lower. Nonetheless, the real or perceived speed

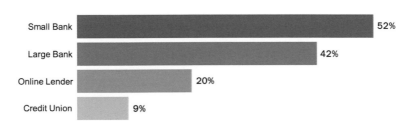

Figure 6.2   20 Percent of Applicants Applied to Online Lenders in 2015
Credit sources applied to (percentage of loan/line of credit applicants)
Source: "2015 Small Business Credit Survey," Federal Reserve Banks, *March 2016.*

of adoption put fintech lenders on the radar of venture capitalists and other early stage investors, and spurred competition.

At the time, we dubbed this period the "wild west," as literally hundreds of new firms—including online lenders, online loan marketplaces, and data analysis firms—entered the market. From 2013 to 2015, many argued that online lending would fundamentally disrupt the marketplace and push traditional banks out of business. Data that already existed, from Yelp reviews to a small business's bank and credit card files to utility bill payment histories, could now be accessed through application programming interfaces (APIs), a major development in computer software that allowed for easier and more efficient data sharing. Automated underwriting algorithms offered a lower cost (and potentially higher quality) innovative replacement for expensive personal underwriting activities. The combination of access to new data and novel underwriting formulas enabled online lenders to start taking market share. In Schumpeterian terms, it appeared that creative destruction would occur as the "takeoff" phase gained steam.

"Takeoff" Aborted

Despite this momentum, the small business lending innovation cycle took a surprise blow in the summer of 2016. An internal probe at Lending Club, one of the leading online lenders, revealed that the company had failed to disclose information to an investor regarding a loan pool. The Lending Club board responded by firing the charismatic CEO and founder, Renaud Laplanche.[17] OnDeck, which had gone public with a valuation of over $1 billion and a share price of $20, saw its stock price plummet by 42 percent between December 2015 and July 2016.[18] Concerned industry observers also began to question whether the new entrants had truly brought disruptive innovation to the market, or had simply made the application experience faster and more pleasant for borrowers. Were online lenders offering new products or were they just offering the same loans and lines of credit processed more quickly and at a higher cost to the borrower?

In the 2015 Fed credit survey, some troubling information about the price of those online loans also emerged. While borrowers generally expressed satisfaction with the ease of the online lending experience, they complained about the high costs and hidden fees (Figure 6.3).

Anecdotes about small businesses falling into debt traps began to appear in the media, and concerns about "bad actors" found their way into the halls of Congress and the offices of regulators. More questions arose: were the new algorithms actually better predictors of small business credit than the bank

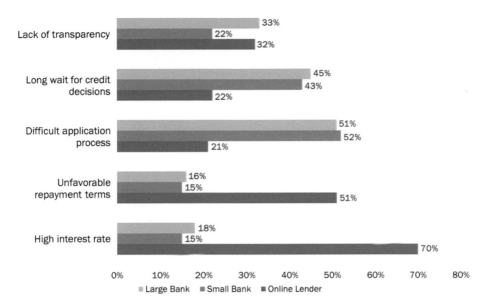

Figure 6.3   Borrowers' Reasons for Dissatisfaction by Lender Type
Percentage of employer firms dissatisfied with lender in 2015
Source: "2015 Small Business Credit Survey," Federal Reserve Banks, *March 2016.*

underwriting models? Were they even as good? And, if the innovation was just in the customer experience, why couldn't banks replicate these processes? Were they just a bunch of "dinosaurs," unable to adapt to change? Most importantly, who held the competitive advantage?

Ferment—Part II

Thus began a second phase of the small business innovation cycle, or perhaps a mini-cycle of further fermentation. The original development of a technology and Internet-enabled front-end application process was so appealing to the small business owner that it jolted the industry into a new era. But, at this point, there was little innovation in the loan products that were delivered. In fact, the products were arguably worse—at least in terms of their cost to borrowers—primarily due to the competitive disadvantages of the new players.

For one, the new online lenders had trouble finding customers. Small business owners are busy and, despite the appeal of a faster experience, online lenders found that placing targeted ads on Google was not enough to reach this fragmented customer base. Beyond just reaching small businesses, the online lenders also needed to get their ads in front of the borrower at almost exactly the moment when they were ready to borrow. As a result, acquiring customers was like finding a needle in a haystack. Customer acquisition costs reached about 15 percent of revenue, some of which was passed back to borrowers in the cost of the loans.

In addition, the new fintech entrants had little track record of performance and no access to the cheap capital that banks held in the form of deposits. Many were using high-cost money from hedge funds to finance their loans. Peer-to-peer lenders played matchmaker, for a fee, between eager borrowers and the individuals and institutions that wanted returns. The unit economics of the innovators, that is, their ability to make profit on a per loan basis, were proving to be a challenge.

At the same time as the early players were stumbling, the dinosaurs were waking up. The established banks and other lenders saw their customers enjoying the ease of the faster and friendlier customer experience, and decided they needed to respond. At first, many just tightened their timelines for responding to loan applications. Turnaround times went from weeks or even months to 10 to 14 days. Processes were still partly manual, but the banks worked on incremental improvements to create fewer burdens for the applicant. This alone made a difference to many small businesses, who finally found more responsive loan officers with a sense of urgency at the other end of the phone. In the months that followed, many banks, even some of those least prone to embracing change, came to realize that they too could use technology to automate small business lending, either by partnering with the new fintech challengers or by beating them at their own game.

Each bank had its own strategy for testing the fintech waters. JPMorgan Chase took early action, partnering with OnDeck in 2015 to deliver an automated small business loan product "white-labeled" under the Chase brand. Wells Fargo developed its own product, called FastFlex, an online fast-decisioned option for small business loans under $100,000 launched in May 2016. Between 2012 and 2017, Citibank invested in more than 20 fintechs to keep an eye on the developing sector and see what innovations might prove worth incorporating. Even community banks engaged, defying the initial view that they would be too small and too technologically backward to explore the new frontiers. Eastern Bank in New England hired a team of fintech entrepreneurs to create Eastern Labs and develop their own in-house small business lending product. After successfully launching Eastern Labs internally, they spun out the technology into its own company, with the purpose of selling the software to other community banks. (Chapter 9 explores the different strategic options available to banks in more detail.)

In the second period of ferment, as the innovation cycle continued to evolve, banks focused on reasserting their leadership in small business lending. Banks realized that they could remain major players because they had at least two important advantages over their fintech competitors. The first advantage was that banks had a pool of customers with whom they already had relationships—and the insights that come from these customers' bank accounts, credit cards, and other bank activities. If a fintech lender like OnDeck could build a company based on data from small business bank accounts, why couldn't the banks that actually hold those accounts use that same data to rebuild their lending processes? The second was that banks had access to lower cost capital in the form of customer deposits. The greatest challenge for the banks would of course be how to change—how to bring new ideas and technologies into a traditional culture in order to better serve their small business customers.

Data and the Entrance of Technology Companies

One of the breakthroughs that enabled the first phase of small business lending innovation was access to data through APIs. Data will also be the driver behind the next set of transformations in small business lending. Big data is increasingly used across multiple industries to better understand customers, competitors, trends, and more. The question is how better data will impact small business lending.

One area is in the credit decision—can the business repay the loan? Additional data to drive better risk assessment could be particularly valuable in small business credit scoring, since small business creditworthiness is difficult to assess due to the heterogeneity and information opacity of small businesses that we discussed earlier. Already, online lenders have begun gathering and analyzing information about small businesses from non-traditional sources. Banks have now begun to look at the bank account payments and credit card activities of their customers to get a more holistic and timely picture of the small business's financial health and ability to repay.

But making the data useful requires algorithms that can utilize it to consistently and accurately predict risk. Although greater availability and multiple sources of data will certainly help, businesses are so different, and their profitability so volatile, that it is not yet clear how to create algorithms that work through the ups and downs of business cycles and maintain accuracy while accounting for the large amount of heterogeneity in small business.

Perhaps the players in the best position to accomplish such a task are large technology platform companies like Amazon and Square. Amazon knows how much the companies on its platform are selling, their cash needs for inventory, and even how their competitors are performing. Square knows their business customers' receipts in real time. These companies also have no issue attracting talented software engineers to build and test new algorithms, while traditional banks often struggle to recruit this talent. And, in contrast to the customer acquisition issues of new fintech start-ups, platforms like Amazon and Square are embedded into the finances and daily operations of many small businesses. They can suggest modifications that seasonality or weather fluctuations might require, and lend the cash to support those investments. Square's MCA products even take their loan repayments from the money that passes through Square's own payment systems, giving them direct access to the collateral that supports their advances.

Reaching "Small Business Utopia"

The early fintech innovators responsible for pushing the small business lending market to a more automated, easy-to-use process may not be the ones to benefit the most from their innovations. This is not unusual. Henry Ford did not invent the automobile, but he dramatically improved the processes by which they were made, and reaped profits and fame as a result. Once told that The Velvet Underground, the seminal 1960s rock band, had only sold 30,000 copies of their debut album, famed musician and producer Brian Eno retorted that "everyone who bought one of those 30,000 copies started a band."[19] Those who change the world do not always profit most from their actions.

The early innovations in small business lending, enabled by entrepreneurs using new sources of data and rethinking the customer experience, have proven not to be the end of the road, but rather, an early stage. It may also be the case that the partnerships between fintechs and banks, and even the improvements banks have made internally, are only incremental though positive steps toward the ultimate small business lending solutions. As in the story of the transistor and the chip, another set of transformative inventions has already become visible—ones that will push this market to achieve its full potential to change the game for small businesses.

We call the end point of this transformation "Small Business Utopia," a state in which the entire financial life of a small business is transformed in a positive way by new technology and innovative tools that meet their needs. In Small Business Utopia, a truly efficient market, operating under appropriate regulatory oversight, will ensure that every creditworthy small business has customer-friendly access to the capital they need to start and grow their business and create jobs.

In addition, this optimal small business environment will give business owners access to new insights on the cash needs of their businesses. This will allow them to be able to take on the right type of capital at the right time, the right price, with the right duration, and use it in a way that maximizes their operating potential. This future state will also benefit lenders, as the costs to make a small business loan will be lower, the risk of default will decrease, and the successful borrower will then likely be a repeat customer for a future loan as their business continues to grow and succeed.

Takeoff: Small Business Lending of the Future

What will be the "chip" of the small business lending story? Platforms such as Amazon, PayPal, and Square will certainly play a role in the new landscape. China has already shown us a model where such actors can dominate. Some traditional players—most notably American Express with its "OPEN" platform, Capital One, and the large banks—with strong small business franchises are also poised to potentially play a role.

But as we move into the next phase of the innovation cycle, there is one additional factor that could determine the winners. The first stages of innovation came from entrepreneurs who saw and understood the pain points of the small business customer. Making the loan experience faster and easier was a breakthrough that got the attention of small businesses and started the chain reaction of industry response. The next phase of innovation will include a solution to another critical small business pain point: the fact that today, there is no tool, no platform, or set of services that provides a small business with a central place to conduct *all* of its financial activity in an integrated, easy-to-use way.

Small businesses often get in trouble because of unexpected cash flow shortfalls. A late customer payment or an unusual inventory need can cause a sudden demand for financing. Most small business owners have low cash buffers. But what if they could see and understand their financial situation and needs more easily? And what if they could borrow the right amount with the right terms at the press of a button? What if they had one dashboard from which to conduct all of their financial activities? Such a platform would include integration of banking activity, cash flow insights and management, and payments processing. It would allow accounting software and tax planning tools to communicate seamlessly with bill paying and retirement planning functions. Artificial intelligence—or even personal advisors—could provide insights and options, based on a holistic picture of the small business.

This is the true vision of Small Business Utopia, where small businesses can run their operations with greater success and longevity. The successful lenders of the future will allow small business owners to better understand what their financing needs are, and access capital quickly and at a competitive and transparent cost. This future may sound distant and difficult to achieve, but the technology required to make it a reality exists today.

Getting to Small Business Utopia will not be easy, in part because many innovations have unintended consequences. Lead was added to paint to make it more water resistant, maintain its color, and dry faster, and added to gasoline to reduce engine knock and boost octane. However, after it became increasingly clear that lead in the environment was a major health hazard, the government began phasing out leaded gasoline in 1974 and banned lead in paint for consumer use in 1978. Even the technological innovations that have allowed us to connect with anyone in the world, get groceries delivered right to our doorstep, and search the web for any information we desire, have also brought with them new issues of data privacy and cybersecurity.

There is abundant evidence that innovation in finance can have negative, or even disastrous, outcomes. The market for over-the-counter derivatives—financial products often used to manage risk that were designed and sold in customized transactions rather than on publicly traded exchanges—grew exponentially in the decade prior to the financial crisis. Many financial firms reaped huge profits through the creation of ever-more-complex products that, in some cases, made the financial system more fragile and vulnerable to collapse. In the fintech innovation cycle, decisions that are rational to individual banks and borrowers may, at the same time, prove collectively destabilizing to the broader financial system. Unfortunately, we have seen the consequences to the economy—and particularly to small businesses—of operating without a well-functioning regulatory structure.

On the other hand, we also have seen that too much or the wrong kind of regulation can impede innovation, particularly in the heavily regulated banking sector. Thus, to achieve the best outcomes, we must develop government policy that promotes innovation while protecting consumers, small businesses, and the financial system.

*   *   *

The innovation cycle in small business lending has gathered steam because technology has delivered new breakthroughs that reduce the long-standing frictions in the ability of new and old lenders to serve the market. In Chapter 7, we describe how the activities of the early fintechs ushered in these changes.

In Chapter 8, we take a further look at the future of small business lending and what a new unified small business financial platform might look like. Given these existing and potential transformations, Chapter 9 explores strategic options for the traditional banks. Finally, Chapters 10 and 11 describe the state of the regulatory system that governs small business lending in the United States, and suggest principles for regulatory reform to increase the likelihood of successfully and safely achieving the heights of the small business lending innovation cycle that these early stages have promised.

The cycle of Schumpeter's creative destruction is only midway through its course. The best results for small businesses lie ahead.

7

The Early Days of Fintech Lending

In June 2013, about 350 people gathered in the Empire Room at Convene Innovation Center in New York to take part in the first ever LendIt conference. Co-founded by Peter Renton, the head of Lend Academy, the one-day event featured a keynote by Lending Club founder and then-CEO Renaud Laplanche. His speech, entitled Transforming the Banking System, told participants that they had the opportunity to emulate disruptive companies such as Netflix and Amazon, and to reshape financial services. Later panel discussions focused on direct and peer-to-peer small business lending models, using better data to make lending safer and more profitable, and exploring why venture capitalists were funding online lending companies. The day ended with a cocktail reception, and the entire event concluded by 7:30 PM.[1,2] Almost all of the small family of fintech lending players attended, but banks and other traditional lenders were notably absent.

The response to this first conference was so positive that Renton and his team turned it into an annual event. In May 2014, the second LendIt conference was a two-day affair that took place at the San Francisco Hilton. Interest had exploded to around 950 in-person attendees and nearly 2,000 watching online. The substance became more specialized, with sessions on small business and short-term lending, loan securitization, peer-to-peer lending in other countries, crowdfunding, and even a Q&A on legal and accounting issues. Significant attention was paid to longer-term industry trends regarding credit underwriting models and the use of big data. Some international fintech issues were touched upon, but most of those were saved for the LendIt conferences in Europe and China that started in 2014 and 2015, and also became annual events.[3]

© The Author(s) 2018
K. G. Mills, *Fintech, Small Business & the American Dream*,
https://doi.org/10.1007/978-3-030-03620-1_7

By 2015, the conference had grown to 2,500 attendees, including banks and credit unions. It featured sessions on "Borrower Acquisition at Scale" and "Partnering with Banks."[4,5] Former U.S. Treasury Secretary and Lending Club board member, Larry Summers, predicted in his keynote that fintechs would take over 70 percent of the small business lending market.[6] The fintech disruption had been launched.

The Frictions of Small Business Lending

Lending to small businesses has always been much more difficult than lending to consumers for two reasons that we have discussed at some length in Part I: the heterogeneity and the information opacity of small firms. Each small business has different characteristics based on industry, location, size, and business goals. Even small business owners themselves are often unsure about what their future cash flows and revenues will look like. As a result, it is difficult to develop a full and nuanced picture of a small business's credit-related metrics: the size of their revenues, when they incur large expenses, how quickly they pay, and how their business is trending. This kind of information makes up what one investor called a "truth file"—a way of capturing the essence of the business's future prospects.[7] For small businesses, developing a truth file has always been notoriously difficult, particularly for smaller and newer firms.

Around 2000, the development of new information interfaces, known as open APIs (application programming interfaces), helped trigger important changes in the quantity and quality of available information on small businesses. An open API is a connection that allows third-party developers to access selected data from a company's site, which can be used to create new applications.[8] In 2000, eBay became one of the first e-commerce companies to use an open API to make extensive information available on small businesses who were selling products on the website. This created a data pipe for online lenders to access information about a small business's eBay sales. The entry of Plaid in 2012 provided a unified API for banking data, which allowed developers to access valuable transaction information and use it to build applications for the fintech ecosystem.[9]

The new backend infrastructure altered some of the longstanding frictions in the small business lending market. With these breakthroughs in data access, online lenders could make better-informed underwriting decisions. In the past, underwriting largely depended on FICO (Fair Isaac Corporation) scores and tax returns, which were not a timely reflection of a business's activity. With new data sources, real-time information once hidden from view or perhaps reported inaccurately by a small business became more visible to underwriters who could use it to better identify creditworthy borrowers.

The First Movers

The fundamental innovation was harnessing the power of the Internet and data, but the incidental innovations were almost as powerful. Enabled by technology and inspired by market need, fintech start-ups brought a new "digital first" approach to online small business lending starting in the late 2000s. This early period lasted through roughly 2013 and was dominated by a few first movers—including CAN Capital, Lending Club, Kabbage, and OnDeck—that each broke new ground in their own way. One common hallmark of the early players was the automated turnaround of online applications that were easy to fill out and created a much better customer experience. These fintechs also brought other new approaches to the market including risk-based pricing, different sources of capital, and twists to traditional products and services.

Risk-Based Pricing

Many credit CAN (Credit Access Network) Capital, founded in 1998, with inventing the merchant cash advance (MCA). The original MCA products relied on a patented technology that allowed credit card receipts to be split between multiple parties.[10] For a small business, this meant that a percentage of its credit card sales could automatically be sent to the MCA provider in order to pay down the advance.

CAN tapped into a market that banks often found too risky: small businesses with urgent cash needs. Since many small businesses experience frequent cash flow fluctuations and have low cash buffers, quick and responsive lenders, even expensive ones, were in high demand. CAN and other MCA lenders were able to extend credit to riskier borrowers using two approaches that traditional banks avoided. First, they used true risk-based pricing, adjusting the interest rate they charged for the perceived risk. Banks have generally had narrow interest rate ranges, pricing loans largely based on what other banks are charging, and assessing risk primarily to make binary decisions about whether or not to lend, as opposed to the rate at which to lend. This has been due in part to the regulatory requirements that govern banks' capital levels. Particularly after the recession, regulatory audits could classify a loan as too risky, and force it to be "qualified" or offset against the banks' capital, making banks reluctant to take on a risky loan asset even if they could theoretically charge a high rate.

The second reason MCA lenders were willing to take on riskier loans was that the structure of the product provided a new and valuable type of collateral. Small business lenders, including the Small Business Administration (SBA), often rely on a personal guarantee from the business owner to provide greater certainty of repayment. In such a case, the bank uses the borrower's assets, often their home, as collateral. Technology allowed MCA lenders to extract loan payments directly from the borrower's bank account or credit card receipts. This technique gave the lender a new kind of collateral—immediate access to customer receipts—rather than waiting for the borrower to make a payment.

Many online lenders followed the structure and pricing levels set by CAN to create pricing for the riskiest loans. The new products were generally priced at a fixed amount. A borrower might receive $10,000 and repay $12,000, by remitting some percentage of daily receipts to the lender as they came in. This was appealing to some small business owners, as their repayment schedule would vary based on actual sales. Business owners also liked knowing the total cost of the loan. But because the schedule to repay the loan was based on sales and not a fixed timeframe, it was nearly impossible to calculate an annual percentage rate (APR) or interest rate before knowing when the loan would be paid back, creating difficulties for small business owners trying to compare the cost of an MCA to that of a traditional loan.[11] With a standard repayment time frame, APR prices could be well north of 30 percent, and even reach 100 percent or more.

New Sources of Capital

Another early fintech was Lending Club, which began as a consumer lending company in 2007. Lending Club was a pioneer of peer-to-peer lending, using technology to bring one of the oldest and most basic forms of consumer lending into the modern world. Like Prosper, another early entrant in consumer loans, peer-to-peer lenders did not make the loans themselves. Instead, they matched individuals and institutional investors willing to provide funding to borrowers seeking capital. By 2010, Lending Club owned 80 percent of the U.S. peer-to-peer lending market.

During its first few years of operation, Lending Club mostly provided consumer loans, reaching $1 billion in loan volume in 2012. The company went public in 2014 with an $8.5 billion valuation, one of the largest IPOs ever for a consumer-facing Internet company.[12] In 2015, Lending Club began to extend credit by matching investors with small business borrowers, providing small-dollar loans between $15,000 and $100,000, with "fixed interest rates starting at 5.9% with terms of one to five years, no hidden fees and no prepayment penalties."[13] Lending Club aimed for ease and simplicity in the loan application process, specifically targeting the painful customer experience that borrowers were getting at banks. In order to sell more of these loans, Lending Club partnered with BancAlliance to gain access to a referral network of hundreds of community banks.[14]

New Data

Another fintech first mover was Kabbage, which launched in 2010. Unlike Lending Club, which began with consumer loans, Kabbage focused on small businesses from the start. Their early business model was to provide working capital loans to eBay merchants, using eBay's newly developed open API to access data on potential small business borrowers and make underwriting decisions.

Kabbage engaged with several partners, including Celtic Bank, using that relationship to scale lending products from the Kabbage platform. Partnerships with Intuit and UPS provided access to customer data to assess creditworthiness, and a partnership with online payment processor Stripe opened up access to more small business customers. Co-founder Kathryn Petralia noted that while Kabbage had started as a niche e-commerce lender, by 2018, a full 90 percent of its business borrowers were offline businesses, and the company had originated a total of $5 billion in loans to more than 130,000 small businesses.[15,16]

Founded in 2006, OnDeck also set out to provide small business credit using a proprietary credit scoring system, known as OnDeck Score. This system integrated public records, accounting, and social data in addition to personal credit scores.[17] In 2012, at a small business lending conference held by the SBA and the U.S. Department of the Treasury (Treasury), OnDeck told the gathering that it was using bank account data to obtain real-time information on small business transactions. This announcement sent a signal to lenders: why use historical data if one could determine creditworthiness in real time? OnDeck went public in 2014 with a $1.3 billion valuation, and in 2015 they began offering credit lines and long-term loan products.[18] By 2018, OnDeck touted itself as the largest online small business lender in the United States, having issued over $8 billion in small business loans.[19]

As with Lending Club and Kabbage, OnDeck's proprietary creditworthiness score could only have been created through APIs that provided access to data from non-traditional sources. In a 2018 interview, LendIt co-founder Peter Renton remarked on how the first movers had set the stage for the fintech revolution. "The data that Kabbage was getting from UPS, eBay, etc., and how they were using it to make predictions—this had never been done before," said Renton. "This was brand new intelligence. There has always been data available, but no one knew how to use it until Kabbage and OnDeck came in and pulled it together."[20]

The Small Business Lending Ecosystem—Circa 2015

The success of the early entrants did not go unnoticed. From 2013 to 2015, dozens of new firms entered the small business online lending ecosystem. The space changed so rapidly that it didn't even have a fixed name. Sometimes the sector was called marketplace lending, reflecting the early success of Prosper, Lending Club, and other peer-to-peer lenders, while at other times, it was called online, alternative, or fintech lending.

The entrants active in this period fell into six categories. There were four types of lenders: balance sheet, peer-to-peer, platform players, and invoice and payables financers. In addition, there were multi-lender marketplaces where small businesses could shop for and compare lenders and their products, and firms that provided data to the other players in the ecosystem (Figure 7.1).

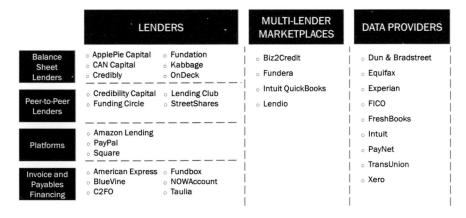

Figure 7.1   Small Business Fintech Lending Ecosystem in 2015
Source: Author's analysis based on Jackson Mueller, "U.S. Online, Non-Bank Finance Landscape," Milken Institute Center for Financial Markets, curated through May 2016.

Balance Sheet and Peer-to-Peer Lenders

Balance sheet lenders included those offering MCA products and one to two-year term loans. These companies held the loans on their firm's balance sheet. Peer-to-peer lenders, by contrast, matched interested investors with potential borrowers. They dominated the early fintech landscape, particularly in the United Kingdom, where government support for new lenders increased following the financial crisis. One particularly strong U.K. entrant was Funding Circle, a small business-focused peer-to-peer lender that entered the U.S. market in 2013 through a merger.[21]

Platform Players

Although they grew to be critical players in online lending, platform lenders did not enter the emerging market until 2011 and their efforts did not gain momentum until a couple of years later. The most visible platform, Amazon, launched Amazon Lending in 2011 and, by the summer of 2017, they were lending $1 billion annually to small businesses with loans ranging from $1,000 to $750,000.[22,23] With the clear potential to expand into other products and services, they became the player to watch. PayPal launched PayPal Working Capital in 2013 and, by 2017, they had lent a total of $3 billion to small businesses.[24]

Square had a built-in base of small businesses using their card payment processing device that could be easily attached to a smartphone. Jack Dorsey, Square's founder (and co-founder and later CEO of Twitter) saw that customers needed small amounts of capital to meet their fluctuating cash needs. He also saw the value of the insights that Square could glean from using their proprietary data on businesses' daily cash receipts and the advantage of having first access to the receipts for debt repayment. In 2014, he formed Square Capital and, in 2015, he hired Jacqueline Reses from Yahoo to lead the effort. By 2016, Square had lent $1 billion, with an average loan size of $6000.[25] By 2018, Square Capital was originating almost $400 million in loans per quarter, largely to the underserved segment of extremely small businesses seeking very small loans.[26]

Another important platform player was American Express, which already had a customer base of thousands of small business credit card users, and had built visibility and good will through its Small Business Saturday initiative and the OPEN small business brand. American Express began utilizing its access to sales and payments information to provide capital to qualified American Express credit card users, allowing these small businesses to access short-term financing at a lower interest rate.

Invoice and Payables Financing

Several new companies began providing invoice financing to help businesses with late-paying customers or seasonal cash flow fluctuations. While factoring—a form of lending that allows a business to sell its invoices to a provider and get immediate cash in exchange for a fee—had long existed, the automation of that process allowed it to occur more seamlessly.

Invoice financing solutions are particularly important for small supply chain companies, which play an underappreciated role in the U.S. economy.[27] Recall our example from Chapter 2 of Transportation and Logistical Services (TLS), a trucking company with ten employees outside of Birmingham, Alabama. Now imagine that Coca-Cola, one of its biggest customers, decides to delay their payment terms from 30 days to 60 days. This would create an unexpected cash crunch for TLS. Online invoice financing provides a solution for small suppliers like TLS to get paid more quickly if they need to.

On the other side of this equation, a second set of products such as Working Capital Terms created by American Express, allowed companies to delay a payment by having the platform pay the vendor, with the company taking on the obligation to pay back the money in 30, 60, or 90 days. This product acted like a business credit card, but provided more flexibility in that payments could be made to entities that didn't accept cards, and terms and pricing were more like those of a short-term loan.

Many fintechs and platforms developed innovative invoice and payments solutions including Fundbox, BlueVine, NOWAccount, and C2FO. Some products were classified as loans, while others were not. All of the providers of these products, however, recognized the reduced risk of lending when they had access to a small business's invoices, a strong piece of collateral to back up the advance.

From the perspective of small businesses, for whom late customer payments have long been a potentially life-threatening nightmare, the new innovations provided a large range of more cost effective and accessible options. Traditional factoring companies such as CIT, once the industry leader, were never inclined to create this kind of innovation, and their products were notoriously expensive and difficult to obtain. As we saw with the government's QuickPay program in Chapter 3, timely payments improve cash buffers and small business performance. Thus, the availability of these fintech products might save thousands of small businesses from untimely demise as a result of cash timing gaps.

Marketplaces

Another group of entrants that emerged during this time were the online lending marketplaces. Companies such as Fundera and Lendio offered small businesses the ability to comparison shop for loan products from both banks and alternative lenders. Marketplaces took a referral fee for each loan originated through their site, which proved worthwhile to many fintechs struggling with customer acquisition. Consumer marketplaces for loans and mortgages have long existed, but small business loan comparisons are more difficult as the products have more variability and small business owners often have less clarity about what kind of loan they need. Nonetheless, online small business marketplaces are a much-needed vehicle to create a more transparent, easier to navigate credit experience.

Data Providers

Data providers became an important part of the new technology-enabled lending ecosystem. Xero and FreshBooks began competing with QuickBooks as a software through which small businesses could manage their finances. Yodlee, an account aggregator, provided software to help businesses predict future cash flows and expenses.

Others collected information on the lending industry itself. PayNet gathered data from banks and commercial finance companies to provide insights and credit ratings to the lenders on their platform. Meanwhile, Orchard collected and shared data about the new fintech players, tracking the number of companies and loan originations, and providing advanced analytics on the nascent industry.[28] These providers developed important information streams for both banks and online lenders, as well as policymakers and regulators.

Small Business Online Lending Appeared Poised for Takeoff

By 2015, online lenders were originating around $5 billion annually in small business loans.[29] Morgan Stanley predicted that these firms would comprise 16.1 percent of the small business lending market by 2020, but that banks would not be at risk, losing only 4.6 percent of their origination volume. The company also predicted that a significant amount of the growth in online lending volumes—$35 billion—would come from expanding credit to underserved borrowers.[30] The new entrants would have plenty of room to grow by

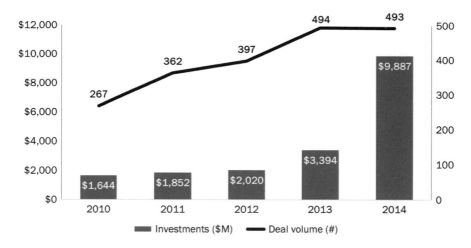

Figure 7.2   Venture Capital Investment in Fintech by Year
Source: "Fintech Investment in U.S. Nearly Tripled in 2014, According to Report by Accenture and Partnership Fund for New York City," Accenture, June 25, 2015, Accenture analysis of CB Insights data.

addressing the market gap in small business lending, particularly the small-dollar loans that banks did not want to make.

During this time, venture capital investment in fintech skyrocketed, growing by almost 200 percent between 2013 and 2014 alone, reaching nearly $10 billion across 493 deals (Figure 7.2).[31]

The new fintech small business lending market seemed poised for takeoff—the phase of the innovation cycle in which volume accelerates and new customers jump into the marketplace, leaving behind old products and companies. Yet, despite the investment and the hype, this expected jump did not occur. What happened instead was another cycle of innovation. This time, the incumbent banks and other new entrants—namely platform companies—took the lead, developing new products and approaches based on their competitive strengths.

Organizational theorist Geoffrey Moore described discontinuous innovations as those that force us to modify our behavior or modify other products and services we rely on.[32] But, he added, "truly discontinuous innovations are new products or services that require the end user and the marketplace to dramatically change their past behavior, with the promise of gaining equally dramatic new benefits."[33] During this period, fintech innovations changed the markets for established financial products but, for several reasons, they would not prove to be "truly discontinuous."

The early movers in the fintech space had shaken up the industry by using new information sources and technology to deliver lending products in a way that was highly automated. From the perspective of the small business owner, the customer experience was significantly better, particularly in terms of speed. But in other important ways, there had been little real innovation in the actual products. With many of the offerings characterized by high prices and low transparency, small businesses began raising concerns about bad actors in the market. Cracks in the fintech success story began to appear.

Challenges to Online Small Business Lenders

By 2017, the industry's underlying issues had caught up to the nascent fintech companies. Rosy predictions about the future of online small business lending were on the decline. This was due, in large part, to a growing realization that many of the innovations brought by the new fintechs could be imitated by incumbent banks, as well as concerns over the advantages that large platform players could exercise if they chose to enter the market.

It started to become clear that both incumbents and disruptors had advantages and disadvantages, and that the winners would be the group that could most quickly and effectively address their shortcomings. Comparing the incumbent players (large banks like JPMorgan Chase and Wells Fargo and smaller community banks) with the new fintech entrants, it became apparent that no one was the clear winner. Instead, it was a pretty mixed picture (Figure 7.3).

Existing banks had the large pools of customers that fintechs were struggling to find. The 2015 annual reports of OnDeck and Lending Club showed that sales and marketing efforts were among the largest operating expenses for both lenders, at about 24 percent and 40 percent of gross revenue,

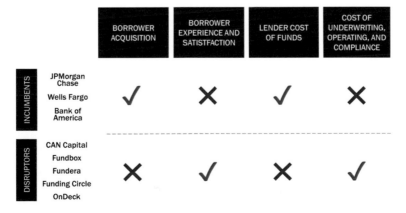

Figure 7.3   Incumbents and Disruptors: Advantages and Disadvantages
Source: Author's analysis based on "The Brave 100: The Battle of Supremacy in Small Business Lending," QED Investors and Oliver Wyman, 2015.

respectively.[34] On a per-loan basis, average costs to acquire a customer were estimated to be $2,500 to $3,500 per loan.[35] As a comparison, in 2017, regional New England lender Eastern Bank reported an average marketing cost of $500 per small business loan under $100,000.[36]

Banks also had access to low cost deposits, while online lenders were largely forced to rely on capital markets to fund loans. Yield-seeking individuals and hedge funds were early sources of capital, but they were expensive and soon dried up as the Federal Reserve began to raise interest rates and the real level of risk in some fintech loans became apparent.

In the early days, the lack of federal regulatory oversight of non-bank lenders was perceived to be an advantage. Banks were reeling from increased compliance costs caused by Dodd-Frank, leading many to predict that the disruptors would see large benefits from "regulatory arbitrage." However, the lack of federal oversight was a double-edged sword. The inability of non-banks to obtain a federal charter may have actually inhibited the national growth of online lenders, as they were forced to charter themselves state by state, use a bank partner, or create products that did not qualify as loans.

The early fintechs had clearly initiated innovations that reduced some of the barriers to a smoother matching of borrowers and lenders in the small business marketplace. They created an advantage by using technology to deliver an easier, faster digital customer experience, but it was unclear whether that advantage was sustainable. Although fintechs were the first to catch on, there was nothing preventing incumbent banks from imitating or even beating them at their own game.

By 2018, the market was consolidating, as peer-to-peer lending stopped growing, and traditional banks increasingly incorporated fintech innovations via acquisition, imitation, or partnership. Perhaps that is why the mood at LendIt 2018 was less exuberant than when it started in 2013, and why the conference had diversified by adding an entire track dedicated to blockchain technology.

*   *   *

Despite the stops and starts, the fintech innovation cycle was underway. The early movers had shown that it was no longer acceptable for banks and other lenders to provide the same small business products and service levels they had for the past several decades. Small businesses had gotten a taste of a new level of service and were in search of more. The stage was set to see how technology might change the game—how additional innovations from current players or future entities might serve the financial needs of small businesses in novel ways that were affordable, integrated, and intelligent.

8

Technology Changes the Game: Small Business Utopia

On a Thursday morning at 5:30 AM, Alex sipped her latte, her elbows atop the service counter. Each day at this time, the sunlight through the front window blanketed her coffee shop and she enjoyed a few moments of peace and quiet before the morning rush began. With 30 minutes to spare before she corralled her baristas for their morning pep talk (and shot of espresso), she unlocked her iPad and pulled up her most valuable assistant: her small business dashboard. A graph on the upper right predicted her cash position at the end of the week. After payroll expenses, she would have $5,000 left over. In seconds, Alex's supply advisor scoured her accounts, sales and expense histories, local weather forecasts, event information, and past tourism data, and told her she would need five new sets of filters and 1,000 plastic cups for the coming week. She ordered them from Amazon with a single touch. She also knew the shop needed a new espresso machine, but she had been putting it off for over a month. With the savings in her account, she could either order the new machine now or make a payment on the term loan she had taken out two years ago to start the business. If she continued to put off a replacement, the machine could break at any moment, and espresso was the second-best selling item on the menu after iced coffee. On the other hand, she was almost done paying off her loan, and procrastinating another month would add interest.

Alex asked her robo-adviser for advice. "You can do both," it reported. "Given your expected sales for the month, it looks like you'll be able to use your savings to pay down the loan and put the espresso machine on your credit card, which has available credit of $3,500. When the credit card payment comes due in 30 days, you will have the cash to pay it off, based on current sales projections."

© The Author(s) 2018
K. G. Mills, *Fintech, Small Business & the American Dream*,
https://doi.org/10.1007/978-3-030-03620-1_8

Alex ordered the espresso machine and paid down the loan, and for good measure, she delayed paying herself for a week, knowing she had enough money in her savings and that sales would jump next week, when the school year ended and summer vacation began. Just to make sure there were no mistakes, she ran an instant credit check on herself, in which her bank bot confirmed she had $3,500 of available credit, and then she double-checked her projected sales based on prior years. Remembering that Dunkin' Donuts had recently opened down the street, Alex asked her bot for sales ideas to ensure they met their goals for the first week of summer vacation.

"It is going to be above 75 degrees next week, so iced coffee, which has a profit margin of 53 percent will likely sell more than usual. Dunkin' Donuts is running a sale on iced coffee next week. When they have run similar promotions in the past, you have lost an average of seven of your daily customers. If you send your regular customers a coupon for $1 off iced coffee, I estimate you will increase your margin for next week by 3 percent. Would you like me to send an e-coupon to your regular customers now?" With one tap, the coupons were sent. After the morning pep talk with her staff, Alex opened the doors for the day, confident in where her small business was headed.

At the end of the day, as Alex was closing up, her bot reminded her that it was June 1, and that quarterly taxes would soon be due. She momentarily worried that she had overlooked her tax payments when buying the new espresso machine, but then the bot said, "Don't worry. Your estimated tax payments have already been accounted for in your cash projections for June." Finally, with a few more taps and swipes, Friday's payroll was set, healthcare deductions were taken from her employees' paychecks, and taxes were ready to file.

Small Business Utopia

Alex's story allows us to imagine a potential golden age of small business financial services that fintech innovations could deliver for small business owners. We call this future state "Small Business Utopia." Alex has access to the capital she needs to operate and grow her business, she can easily understand her cash flow, and she has real-time insight into customer acquisition and sales techniques that can help her business prosper. In this story, a machine augments Alex's ability to run her business through artificial intelligence that collects a range of data, knows how to assess and learn from it, and can answer our protagonist's questions about her business's financial situation.

In consumer lending, it is easy to imagine this world. We already have mobile banking apps that tell us our FICO (Fair Isaac Corporation) scores, credit availability, and how much we are spending each month. A platform that integrates all these capabilities is likely to emerge in the future, and might even include robo-advice about taking out a mortgage or when to refinance student debt.

The future for small business will not look quite like the consumer environment because the needs of small business owners are different. A "smart" environment of the future will integrate the disparate sources of information a small business owner currently has to wade through manually. Accounting software, bank balances, credit cards, tax payments, and bank loans all exist today in their own information streams. It is left to the small business owner, or her advisor or accountant, to integrate them and draw out the implications for cash balances and business decisions. The technology exists, or will soon be available, to meld this information onto a single platform. Imagine an intelligent virtual assistant that relies on a range of automated features and predictive formulas, all serving to compile and sort through the vast array of available data and anticipate a small business's future sales and cash requirements.

Reaching this state of Small Business Utopia will involve getting three factors right. First, technology will need to make information streams about small businesses more readily available and integrate them in ways that illuminate the small business's financial health and future needs. Second, credit or other appropriate loan products need to be easily available to the small business borrower. This requires lenders to refine their expertise in determining who is creditworthy. Third, to be successful, the new environment must be built around the needs of small businesses, rather than a consumer concept that is simply modified for small businesses. In the past, all three conditions were hard to meet. Today, they may be within our reach.

A Platform to Rule All Others

In the story of Alex and her coffee shop, she comes to work and logs into one system, her small business dashboard. This dashboard does not exist for small businesses today. Instead, a business owner has one system, perhaps QuickBooks or Xero, for their accounting software, one portal for bank transactions, another like HubSpot for marketing, and a separate payroll system such as ADP or Gusto. In addition, there is a separate healthcare or benefits portal and taxes are often paid offline.

Ask small businesses about their concerns and they often mention their worries about forgetting to make a quarterly payroll tax payment or coming up short because they neglected to put away the cash that they will owe. They fear that they have not planned well for seasonal cash needs, when they have to pay for a big order of inventory, or when a large customer pays late. In a large business, enterprise resource planning (ERP) systems take care of cash forecasting, based on an integrated platform that draws on sales systems, supply chain systems, and manufacturing and product data.

A similar system for small businesses would combine at least four key activities: banking and payments, loans and credit, accounting, and tax. The key to the dashboard's value would be to give more visibility into a business's future cash flows. One can see the value of knowing more precisely when future lean periods or shortfalls might be coming up, and having the opportunity to set aside a rainy day fund. This transparency into future cash flows could benefit a growing business by giving it the confidence to make a large investment decision, such as expanding or buying new equipment. In this "utopian" world, fewer good businesses might fail, and more businesses would have the confidence and financial resources to grow successfully.

A cash flow dashboard would not just benefit the small business owner. It would also create valuable information flow for a lender. Today, lenders such as Amazon, American Express, and Square rely on transaction data from their platforms. But for small businesses that do not sell at retail, lenders do not yet have the equivalent real-time data on their prospects. A platform that provides an intelligent combination of revenue, receipts, orders, payments to suppliers, and other expenses would help a lender provide credit at the push of a button. Businesses could proceed more securely, knowing they had greater cash buffers, and lenders would have the benefits that cash flow transparency lends to the underwriting and risk assessment process.

The basic technology to create a connected dashboard exists today. Why, if it is what small businesses want, has it not been developed? Today, each data stream lives within the purview of a different provider (e.g. TurboTax or Visa), each of which may or may not be inclined to provide access. Some of the data, such as banking information, is not controlled by the business owner. This is why Open Banking initiatives in Europe and the United Kingdom, which gave ownership of banking data to consumers and small businesses, were so momentous. (Open Banking and its implications are discussed further in Chapter 11.)

There is no question, however, that small business intelligence will develop quickly on the coattails of other areas of big data and artificial intelligence. Combining data sources and using analytic techniques to understand patterns and create predictions is happening already in numerous areas such as marketing and customer acquisition. These same capacities will be the foundational elements for creating an intelligent small business financial platform or dashboard.

Big Data, Predictive Modeling, and Artificial Intelligence

During our interviews, we heard a story about a man in Shanghai who used Alipay, a payment application developed by the technology platform Alibaba, to buy his coffee. As he sat down to drink his coffee, he received a notification on his smartphone, providing him with a map of his predicted route (based on his previous travel to the area), and notifying him that he would receive 10 percent discounts at two small businesses along his path. In the United States, iPhones have begun to more subtly provide this kind of information, directing you "home" using the route with the least traffic and predicting locations where you may want to stop along the way. Facebook has a feature that provides users with a list of nearby restaurants they might like whenever they arrive in a new city. We have become accustomed to seeing ads on Google and Amazon based upon our search history.

One large U.K. bank told us the story of a client, a small seaside hotel looking to understand its customers. The bank had extensive information on a large share of the hotel's customer base, because many of those customers had used the bank's credit card to pay for their stay. The bank could provide anonymized data and intelligence about the hotel's clientele—how far they had traveled or what other food or activities they preferred—which helped the hotel develop better customer-focused services and marketing plans.

The ultimate small business dashboard of the future will combine intelligence from a business's past activity (i.e. sales, purchases, etc.) with predictions and marketing advice, producing a business-savvy bot like the one in Alex's coffee shop. If the projected business trends show a cash need for investment or routine cash fluctuations, the owner may wish to seek a loan or line of credit. This intelligent bot would be able to help the small business owner access credit more seamlessly, comparing available options and recommending drawdowns on credit as needed.

For the bot we have imagined to work, the market for small business credit needs to be much more transparent and efficient than it is today. The future state requires more standardized and clearly defined loan products, and crisp credit standards so a small business knows quickly and exactly how much credit might be available to them. Small business credit marketplaces such as Fundera and Lendio have made some strides in this direction. In addition, the emergence of standardized, automated credit formulas is pushing small business lending toward a state where a small business might have a well of existing credit that they can draw from at their disposal, like a credit line on a business credit card. Eventually, this credit would be visible on an intelligent small business platform and accessible at the push of a button.

The Role of Big Data in Establishing Creditworthiness

The availability of new and large sources of data is not just helpful to the small business owner in managing their business and predicting their credit needs. Big data is also changing the way lenders make credit decisions. The use of data started slowly as fintechs emerged. One of the most important breakthroughs was actually fairly mundane: the idea that OnDeck pioneered of using current activity from a business's bank account as a timelier indicator of whether a business was creditworthy. A business that was paying its rent and suppliers on time was likely a better loan prospect than one who was behind and missing payments. Other data streams, such as Yelp reviews, looked interesting, but initial algorithms struggled to find good results with these novel indicators. This may be changing, as the possibilities of using data from new sources, such as mobile phones, are nearly endless. (See box)

Unlocking Credit with an Android App

Tala Mobile, a company specializing in making micro-loans to individuals and small businesses in the Philippines, Kenya, Tanzania, and Mexico, pulls data from the mobile devices of its users, converts it into a scalable format, and uses it to analyze a business owner's behavior and likelihood to repay. With the customer's permission, Tala gains access to a massive amount of information through its Android application, including merchant transactions, call logs, receipts, and other predictive data. Tala uses the information not only to determine the creditworthiness of the business owner, but also to assist them in developing their business plan and managing cash flow.

Focusing its work in underserved communities, where potential customers are often unseen due to their lack of credit history, Tala has been able to succeed using this new data source and innovative approach to assessing credit. Since its founding in 2012, Tala has provided 7 million loans to more than 1.5 million people in five countries across three continents. The company loaned $350 million in just under three years while still maintaining a write-off rate of under 7.5 percent.[1]

The story of Tala Mobile is not an isolated example. Many traditional and new lenders, from large banks to platform players like Amazon and Google, have large amounts of data that can be used to generate information about what kind of loan a small business needs and when, as well as what the business can do to increase its sales and otherwise improve its financial situation.

The potential uses of big data, predictive algorithms, and other kinds of artificial intelligence are both exciting and scary. As with all advances, there is a lot of potential downside in the future world we have imagined for small businesses and their lenders. One significant risk is the possibility of unintended consequences, or even potential misuse of data, as a result of algorithm-driven decision-making.

Imagine a car insurance company that sifted through its customer data and identified a single factor that consistently correlated with a 30 percent increase in car accidents. Now imagine that the factor was whether the driver of the car bought frozen pizza. This example may seem absurd, since there is no obvious causal link between frozen pizza-buying behavior and auto accidents, but it is based on a true story. The real insurance company in the example decided not to use the data to determine their insurance premiums for two reasons. First, if people found out that buying frozen pizza would hike their premiums, they would stop buying it without changing the other risk factors that actually caused accidents. Second, the company felt that its use of the information, if known, would likely provoke a public backlash.

But what if the insurance company had made the opposite decision or a small business lender used similar data to determine loan approvals and pricing? What recourse would the small business owner have if they were suddenly refused credit? Would the business have the right to a transparent review of the data used to make the decision? Who controls the algorithm?

These questions are pertinent as we think about the next phase of innovation in financial technology. In the United Kingdom, regulators have implemented an Open Banking regime, which facilitates data sharing across financial entities and in which small businesses and consumers own their financial data.[2] Their experience will begin to test important questions, such as who can use data and how, and perhaps, most importantly, what happens when lenders increasingly move from pre-programmed algorithms to machine learning.

A Black Box

In 2000, Google co-founder Larry Page said that, "Artificial intelligence would be the ultimate version of Google. The ultimate search engine that would understand everything on the web. It would understand exactly what you wanted, and it would give you the right thing. We're nowhere near doing that now. However, we can get incrementally closer to that, and that is basically what we work on."[3]

It is easy to imagine a dark side to the advances in artificial intelligence. In March 2016, inventor David Hanson brought his newest gadget to an interview with CNBC. What followed stunned the world, as Sophia, a lifelike robot built in the image of Audrey Hepburn, responded to Hanson's question of "Do you want to destroy humans?" by saying, "OK. I will destroy humans."[4] Technology entrepreneur Elon Musk warned, "I'm increasingly inclined to think that there should be some regulatory oversight, maybe at the national and international level, just to make sure that we don't do something very foolish. I mean with artificial intelligence we're summoning the demon."[5]

Economists have begun to explore the implications of artificial intelligence on innovation. They view artificial intelligence as a "general purpose technology," which, like the semiconductor in our innovation story, has the potential to create significant advances in multiple industries.[6] Artificial intelligence has the possibility of becoming a powerful enabler of innovation because it is actually an "invention of a new method of invention."[7] These economists also suggest that the winners are going to be those who have control over large amounts of unstructured data.

This raises a potential risk of artificial intelligence. If certain companies are allowed to have a monopoly over collections of data, this could adversely affect future innovation and the shared benefits it would bring. As we will discuss further in Chapter 11, future regulation needs to ensure that there is open access to data streams to power better insights for small businesses and other sectors.

In addition, as machines learn to identify who is more likely to default on their loans, the risk of discrimination and exclusion becomes significant. Most worrisome is the idea that data would be analyzed in a "black box"; that no one would know exactly what the machine was using to make recommendations or decisions. So, while the insurance company in our previous example could deliberately decide not to include frozen pizza purchases in its algorithm, a machine could discover the same correlation and—barring explicit rules preventing it from doing so—include it as a pricing factor. By the same token, a machine might identify a risk factor that happens to correlate strongly with race, gender, or the characteristics of other protected classes. Machines that lack intuition and situational awareness could create serious problems.

Black box models are not un-auditable; they're just incomprehensible, but it is possible that artificial intelligence could make them comprehensible and monitor or control them. Both companies and regulators will need to develop new technological methods to untangle the inner workings of the algorithms of the future. Even if automation is developed that is capable of detecting discrimination and other bad outcomes, it seems likely that human oversight of these important issues at companies and by regulators will be required as well.

The Small Business Bank of the Future

Traditionally, small business loans and services have been conducted by banks that also serve consumers, do real estate transactions, and have other important lines of business. The idea of a bank or other financial entity focusing exclusively on small business is a somewhat novel concept in the financial services market. Yet, such an entity will likely have a competitive advantage in developing the small business dashboard and associated integrated credit activities we have described.

The small business dashboard and the intelligence that powers it do not have as much in common with consumer systems as one might think. A consumer might be focused on repaying student loans, consolidating credit card debt, or planning for college, a vacation, or retirement. Although there are analogs in the world of small businesses, their basic activities and worries are different. The concerns of small business owners revolve around the inner workings of their business: if it is making a profit and whether the cash flows match the required payments.

Another way for a bank to specialize even further is to cater to a particular subset of small businesses differentiated by their industry, geography, or size. Given the heterogeneity of small businesses, such a focus might be a winning formula. Live Oak, a forward-thinking bank founded in 2008, began by lending almost exclusively to veterinarians. They followed on with funeral homes and chicken farms. This early specialization gave them unique insights into the particular activities and creditworthiness of each chosen small business segment. Kabbage began with online eBay sellers. Other lenders have specialized in women or minority-owned businesses or government contractors.

The small business bank of the future may not even be a bank in the sense we think of them today. It could be an online entity that conducts its transactions through a traditional bank, or it could be one of the current platform players such as Amazon, or a financial services competitor such as American Express, Capital One, or Visa. The beauty of the innovative boost that the fintech wave has given to small business lending is that all of these competitors are considering their options. And most are doing it with a new appreciation of the particular needs of their potential small business clients, and a desire to serve them well.

The Future Role of Relationships

It might seem at first that in a new era of technology-enabled underwriting, processing, and advising, there would be no place for relationship lending. But this will not be the case. Small business problems are so particular, and entrepreneurs are so different, that relationships will remain important, if they can be built and maintained affordably.

Community banks have historically held a competitive advantage for small business loans, largely because of their relationships with their small business customers, where they provide advice and counsel. These conversations help create customer-product fit—getting the small business a loan of the right amount, the right duration, and the right cost, so they can successfully use it for the intended purpose and repay it. Under pressure to improve their profit margins, community banks have been forced to move away from relationships, particularly with the smallest businesses, as these personal activities are costly to build and maintain.

Who will fill these needs in the future? The Small Business Administration does an important part of this work, counseling over one million small businesses a year using a vast network of Small Business Development Centers and SCORE volunteers.[8,9] Community Development Financial Institutions (CDFIs) have historically provided access to credit to underserved borrowers through personal relationships and advice.[10] They are valuable players, but they cannot meet the marketplace's needs given their limited funding.

The answer is likely that both human and artificial intelligence in combination will provide a new set of solutions. The small business owner can use automated intelligence to understand their needs and get credit as their situation permits. But they also will need access to a personal conversation or relationship, to help them make more complicated decisions.

JPMorgan Chase has taken this two-fold approach. In addition to billions in fintech investments, they are investing in face-to-face services. In 2018, the bank announced it would open 400 additional branches and launched the Chase for Business BizMobile™.[11] This bus parks in a designated area and invites small business owners in to have a conversation about their marketing strategies and financing needs (Figure 8.1).[12]

One could imagine that Alex, our coffee shop owner, would also have the need for a trusted human advisor to supplement the bot that proved so helpful. Although the human advisor could be part of the platform and in a different location, it does seem more useful if they knew the local situation. In

Figure 8.1   Chase for Business BizMobile™
Source: Chase BizMobile teaser, June 14, 2018.

an optimal future small business ecosystem, new intelligence for small business owners, easily accessible loan products, and human advice and counsel will all be part of the mix.

*   *   *

The small business bank of the future might be a large or small bank that is already part of the landscape today—it may be a platform or fintech lender, or it may be a new entity that does not currently exist. There may only be a few of these "banks" or there may be many, each serving different industries. As the innovation cycle progresses, a shakeout process will likely occur along the way, where the successful firms will be those that understand the needs of small businesses and serve them in a streamlined way. Thus, in this future state, small businesses will be the ultimate winners.

9

A Playbook for Banks

It was a cold, winter day in January 2017 as Eastern Bank CEO Bob Rivers stared out the window overlooking downtown Boston, reflecting on Eastern's recent innovation adventures. Rivers had just become Eastern Bank's Chairman and CEO, starting his career as a bank teller 35 years earlier and working his way up through the ranks in several banks, before becoming Eastern's President in 2007. Rivers had seen the signs of disruption—technology seemed to be taking over the world and banking was no different. Now the bank was at the end of a three-year internal innovation project designed to bring new technology solutions to its customers. Eastern Labs had developed a hugely successful, fully automated small business lending product that was recognized as an industry leader, and had strong adoption by Eastern customers.

Rivers was proud of what they had accomplished. Eastern Bank was by all accounts a traditional bank. Founded in Salem, Massachusetts in 1818, Eastern was the oldest and largest mutual bank in the country. Being a mutual bank meant Eastern had no shareholders, and was instead owned by its depositors—a model that restricted the bank's capital stock to retained earnings. Begun as an attempt by some wealthy New England merchants and ship owners to provide access to capital for those in the community to build homes, Eastern Bank originally opened once a week—on Wednesdays from 12 to 1 PM. It offered a 5 percent passbook account and a precursor to the modern home mortgage. In addition to repaying the principal and the interest on their loans, borrowers incurred one additional "fee." They had to volunteer at the bank in order to help expand the hours. This community focus and the mutual ownership structure had been part of the fundamental identity of Eastern Bank for almost 200 years.

© The Author(s) 2018
K. G. Mills, *Fintech, Small Business & the American Dream*,
https://doi.org/10.1007/978-3-030-03620-1_9

Through most of the 1980s and 1990s, Eastern operated as a traditional community bank, serving the New England region with a large branch network, specializing in small and middle-market business, consumer banking, and insurance brokerage. In 1997, Eastern began a massive expansion push, aiming to double the size of the bank within ten years. More than a decade later, as the nation emerged from the worst financial crisis since the Great Depression, Eastern found itself in a relatively fortunate position. With few risky loans on its books, it had escaped the crisis with minimal losses and without closing a single branch. As the crisis came to an end, Rivers realized that Eastern had the capacity to meet the needs of small businesses whose credit had been constrained during the crisis. As Rivers put it, his team felt they had "both an opportunity and a responsibility to step up." They decided to focus on Small Business Administration (SBA)-guaranteed lending and, within six months of ramping up their small business operation, Eastern was the top SBA lender in Massachusetts, and eventually became a top-10 SBA lender nationally.

But Rivers was still worried. Small business lending was a core part of their business, but fintech disruptors were providing a better customer experience and processing the loans faster than Eastern's manual process would ever allow. Determined to compete, Bob Rivers and Chief Information Officer Don Westermann decided to take a walk around Kendall Square, home to Massachusetts Institute of Technology (MIT), where many of these fintech entrepreneurs were incubating their companies. With few connections in this field, Rivers and Westermann cold called people and took meetings with whomever they could find. Rivers ultimately wanted to find someone to transform Eastern's technology, arguing, "We should worry about people putting us out of business, but we should also put ourselves out of business." One day, Rivers picked up the Boston Globe, and noticed that PerkStreet Financial, an online bank headquartered in Boston, was struggling to make ends meet. Once thought to be the future of banking, PerkStreet was closing after just four years in business. But the talented innovator behind PerkStreet piqued Rivers' interest. He picked up the phone, called his network in Kendall Square, and asked if they could put him in touch with PerkStreet's CEO Dan O'Malley.

By the time Rivers called, O'Malley had already been searching for a bank with whom to partner for about one month. He believed that his project at PerkStreet would have been more easily executed within a bank rather than through an independent entity. After three months of negotiating, O'Malley officially joined Eastern Bank as their Chief Digital Officer, responsible for the bank's product team, customer support, and "Eastern Labs"—the new innovation group located in the lobby of Eastern Bank's headquarters. With a $4 million annual investment from the Board, Eastern Labs began running a series of tests.

Initially, they simply set up a basic web page and used the customer support team to reach potential customers by phone and email. Once a customer applied, their information was processed manually within two hours, cutting turnaround time dramatically without having to build an automated system. As O'Malley said, "We decided to fake it until we made it."

But having an innovation team work inside of a traditional bank was not easy. The process of experimenting with new products was messy and involved risk. For example, in O'Malley's first test, he wanted to run what he called a "universe test," approving loans for anyone who applied just to see if there was a demand for the faster, online process. One team member's response was, "So you want me to open the window, take taxpayer-guaranteed money and just hand it out to anyone who shows up. That's the stupidest idea I've ever heard."

Even those who did not work with Labs felt its influence—after all, they saw it in the lobby every day. Some felt that the money and attention going to Labs could be better spent supporting their day-to-day operations, or on other new projects such as developing the mobile banking application on which they had been previously focused.

Despite all of this tension, Labs developed a successful product. Over three years, $12 million, and multiple tests, a project that began with a basic web page ended with a product that fully automated Eastern's small business lending and improved customer acquisition through digital marketing, all while meeting the bank's regulatory and internal underwriting requirements. O'Malley saw an opportunity to sell the product to other community banks and believed this combination of automated loan processing and improved marketing gave the product unique appeal. As he put it, "Real-time loan origination reduces back office costs but doesn't itself drive growth. Growth comes from automating sales in new [digital] channels." Eventually, O'Malley spun out the product into its own company called Numerated Growth Technologies, in which Eastern Bank had an equity stake.[1]

The Future of Small Business Banking

Eastern Labs was seen as a success story, and other small banks started to take notice. If a 200-year-old mutual bank could innovate like this, perhaps they could, too. Or perhaps they could take a product like Numerated and integrate it into their existing systems. Banks also began to realize that the processes being digitized were processes that already existed within their own institutions. While the impetus to automate them may have come from the outside, banks had a range of options to adapt, from building their own new products to partnering with a fintech company.

One of the key attributes that helped Eastern Bank succeed is that they had long focused on serving small businesses. As banks think about the future of small business lending, it will no longer be enough for them to treat small business lending as an add-on to their consumer business or a subdivision of their larger commercial lending departments. The successful small business lenders of the future will make small business its own area, creating the customer experiences and innovative products that small businesses will see from new competitors, and come to expect and demand.

If a bank does want to become a "small business bank of the future," there are a number of ways in which they can acquire the expertise and technology necessary to compete. Around the same time as the Numerated spin out was happening, there was an explosion of partnerships between fintechs and banks. In December 2015, JPMorgan Chase led the way by announcing a partnership with OnDeck under the Chase brand.[2,3] This was not an easy process and it took more than a year for JPMorgan to complete the partnership, due to the technical requirements of systems integration and third-party regulations that required OnDeck to be compliant with bank vendor standards. The arrangement was viewed by many as a brilliant move. JPMorgan Chase gained access to the technology and expertise of one of the leading fintech players without paying billions of dollars to acquire OnDeck, which had gone public with a large valuation just a year earlier. And in another win for the bank, Chase was the brand giving the small businesses this new level of service. However, others saw this effort as a mistake, including some inside the bank. Why not create their own innovative product as Wells Fargo had? And why put so much time and energy into such a small segment of their overall lending portfolio? Nevertheless, the investments continued. From 2016 to 2018, as many other banks were adjusting their bearings, JPMorgan Chase pumped more than $20 billion into developing new mobile and digital products and invested in more than 100 fintechs.[4]

Wells Fargo began its foray into the online lending space in May 2016 through its FastFlex small business program. During the initial rollout, loans were only available to existing business customers who had held accounts with Wells Fargo for at least a year. The transactional data the bank already possessed proved invaluable to the underwriting process. FastFlex offered loans starting from $10,000 and up to $35,000, targeting a portion of the small business lending market often overlooked by other traditional banking institutions.[5] Wells Fargo also built out a section of its website dedicated to assisting small businesses. Wells Fargo Works *for Small Business*® offered advice on topics relevant to small businesses, success story videos, business and marketing planning centers, and even a competitive intelligence tool that helped small businesses map out their competitors, customers, and suppliers to determine where best to target their next advertising campaign.[6] These efforts extended the bank's activities, but were not transformative. In 2016, Bank of America launched Erica, a "virtual financial assistant" that could retrieve account information, make transactions, and provide help to the bank's customers using "predictive analytics and cognitive messaging."[7]

The initial efforts of JPMorgan Chase, Wells Fargo, and Bank of America signaled that these banks wanted to play in the new lending environment, but these early templates should not be viewed as the final model. Small business lending markets continue to change rapidly, and merely adding information and tools will not be enough for these important large banks to maintain their leadership.

In this shifting small business landscape, all banks, large and small, face a decision: should they evolve their activities or stick to existing ways, and if they decide to be engaged in innovation, how should they go about it? Should they build a product internally, partner, or buy the new technology? And, how will small business innovation relate to other fintech investments in data access, payments, or artificial intelligence that they might make?

A Playbook for Banks

A surprising number of banks, including many who were smaller and more traditional like Eastern, decided that they were not dinosaurs (as Bill Gates had described them in 1994) and found ways to innovate.[8] Bob Rivers of Eastern Bank saw a benefit in finding a lower-cost, more automated way of delivering small loans, as it allowed the bank to make some profit and maintain the relationship with the business. If a business cannot come to a bank for a $100,000 loan, it is unlikely to come to that bank for the $500,000 loan it needs down the road. Rivers believed that his bank would be in serious financial trouble if it did not innovate in small business lending, which led him to take on big initiatives, like Eastern Labs, even though doing so upset many of the bank's norms and processes.

There is, however, a second line of thinking at many banks: the "not my problem" approach. This stems from the view that the bank does not have the time or capacity to compete with fintech companies, and sometimes operates on an implicit assumption that fintech firms are a passing fad or will not directly compete with banks. For some banks, this approach has meant doubling down on their strengths, including high-cost activities like manual underwriting, believing that the bank's procedures result in better lending decisions than a technology-enabled process would deliver.

Some banks have developed a middle ground, such as Frost Bank in San Antonio, which took an innovative approach without giving up its strong reputation for relationship lending.[9] Frost began offering online mobile products that were well-designed and user-friendly, while maintaining a call system in which customers were directed to a real person, instead of an automated menu. All final loan decisions involved a face-to-face interaction. Frost saw value in maintaining their emphasis on relationship lending, but used technology to reduce costs and make the borrower experience faster and easier.

Questions Banks Should Ask

More generally, framing the question as an "either/or"—either a bank is innovative or it is not—often obscures the larger set of questions that banks should consider when deciding what to do about small business lending. To develop a strategy that fits each bank, we propose asking a new set of questions (Figure 9.1).

First, does the bank even want to serve more small business customers? For some banks, the answer will be no. For others, like Eastern Bank, small business lending is a priority. How might a bank make this decision? On the one hand, small business loans tend to be small and therefore low profit, particularly if the costs to acquire, underwrite, and process the loan are too high. They are also diverse in terms of risk, so a portfolio of small business loans has to be monitored effectively, which can take time and expertise. On the other

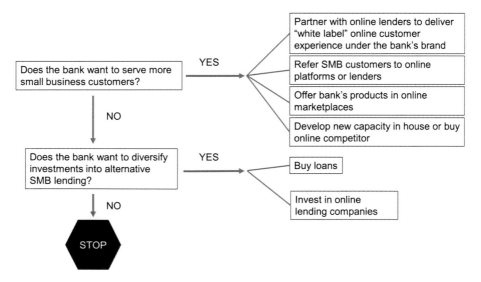

Figure 9.1   Decision Matrix for Banks

hand, making small business loans can be done profitably and allow banks to cross-sell other products to the small business. In the past, it was acceptable for banks to say that small business was a priority, but to put off concrete actions that would improve their small business products and customer experiences because they knew there were few alternatives for small businesses seeking credit. In the emerging, more competitive environment, lip service will no longer be sufficient.

If the answer is "no," the bank does not want to service more small business customers, then the next question is whether the bank wants to hold small business assets on its books, even if they do not provide small business loans themselves. If the answer to this second question is no, there is no need to go any further. However, if the answer is yes, then buying small business loans can be an appropriate strategy for smaller banks. Companies like Community Capital Technology have begun providing a marketplace for smaller banks to buy and sell loans.[10]

Another strategy, more appropriate for larger banks, is to invest in online lending companies as a way to indirectly participate. From 2012 to 2017, Citibank, for example, participated in 30 funding rounds to over 20 fintech companies hoping to both earn some return and monitor interesting developments in the fintech space.[11]

For banks that answer "yes" to wanting to serve more small business customers, there are a range of mechanisms to do so. The first is partnerships, which involve some level of integration with a fintech provider. Banks can use an alternative lender's technology to power an online loan application, often "white labeling" the online application, underwriting, and technology, by branding it with the bank's own marketing. Citizens Bank, for example, partnered with online lender Fundation to provide a digital application and processing for small business loans, with same-day decisions and funding within three days of approval.[12]

Others have copied Citibank and incubated fintech companies in a separate environment, then bought or partnered with those that add value to the bank. Barclays, for example, started the "Rise" program, an effort to attract the best ideas and entrepreneurs to accelerator programs in seven locations, with the tag line, "If you are involved with Fintech, you need to be involved with Rise."[13] This provided a mechanism to monitor industry developments and latch on to the best ones that fit within the bank. In August 2018, Barclays teamed up with MarketInvoice, a tool that helps companies sell their outstanding invoices in exchange for working capital. Barclays obtained a minority stake in the technology platform and announced plans to use the fintech's investor capital and invoice financing capabilities to provide capital to its small and medium-sized businesses.[14]

A second way to serve more small businesses is referrals, in which banks refer declined applicants to online lenders. In the United Kingdom, the government mandated that banks refer declined small business loan applicants to a fintech provider for consideration. Although this has not been very successful in the United Kingdom, some banks and fintechs in the United States have partnered on referrals to help the bank serve more customers. In the Citizens Bank/Fundation partnership, for example, Fundation will sometimes provide loans to small businesses that do not meet Citizens' credit approval criteria.[15]

The third option is offering the bank's small business lending products through an online marketplace. Small businesses are increasingly looking for a central location where they can get access to the growing variety of loan options. Early fintech entrants, Fundera and Lendio, provide a platform on which banks and fintechs can offer lending products to small business customers, who can comparison shop to get the loan that is right for them. These online marketplaces generally reduce customer acquisition costs for lenders and provide potential borrowers with a user-friendly experience. If banks can offer lower interest loans due to their cheaper capital costs or other factors, these channels can also help them compete directly with fintechs in a transparent marketplace.

The fourth option is to develop capacity in-house, as Eastern Bank did. This can be done through incremental innovation or with the goal of transforming the bank. These in-house innovations can range from the automation of existing bank processes to the development of new underwriting methods based on machine learning and alternative customer data, like utility bill payments. Wells Fargo, for example, is pursuing a large innovation project that involves pooling all of its information in a central data lake, and using this resource to create new insights and ultimately improve lending products for small businesses.[16]

With this range of options, how should banks that want to serve more small business customers decide which strategy is right for them? The choice depends largely on how much time and money the bank is willing to invest to enter the new marketplace, and the level of integration the bank wants between the new digital activities and their traditional operations. In other words, the two questions that banks must ask are: "how much time and money do I want to invest?" and "how much integration do I want to have?" The following chart puts the strategic options described earlier into a matrix that explains the level of resource investment and integration associated with each (Figure 9.2).[17]

Making a decision about how much time and money to invest to compete with disruptive innovation requires answering an additional question, "How threatening is innovation to the business?" At Eastern, Bob Rivers thought technology was very threatening. He saw that within a few years of the

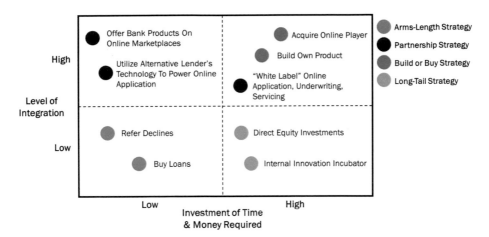

Figure 9.2   Strategic Decisions for Banks

fintechs' emergence, a growing percentage of small businesses were applying online, and they preferred the borrower experience of online lenders to the paperwork-intensive process of banks like Eastern.[18] When he and O'Malley looked into Eastern's small business transaction data, they saw that even the small businesses that banked with Eastern were taking loans from online lenders. This led Rivers to invest 1 percent of Eastern's annual gross revenue into the Labs project and to dedicate a great deal of personal time and attention to Eastern Labs.

Determining how much integration is appropriate requires asking another question: how essential is small business lending to the bank's business? As the regional leader in SBA lending, Rivers knew that small business lending was core to his business. He also knew that if small businesses started going to online lenders instead of to Eastern, it could have implications not only for Eastern's small business lending, but also for all of the other products cross-sold to their small business borrowers. Thus, Rivers decided he needed the small business innovation activity to be highly integrated into his bank. This meant pursuing the high-risk strategy of building his own product. It also meant putting Eastern Labs in the lobby of the bank's headquarters so that the entire organization understood the level of commitment that the CEO wanted to attain.

Innovation in a Traditional Bank

Any innovation inside of a traditional organization, such as a bank, is difficult. Banks tend to have risk-averse cultures, in part because they are heavily regulated and must protect customer deposits. What if the technology doesn't work? What if customers don't like it? What if internal personnel don't want to change? When the management of the traditional business feels threatened by the innovation, they may try to stymie it. (On the other hand, an innovation that is not at all threatening to a core business line is probably tangential to the bank, and may not be worth taking up in the first place.) So how should banks think about structuring whatever innovation activity they decide to pursue?

One prominent theory of organizational behavior suggests initially separating the innovative activity from the day-to-day operations of the business, creating an "ambidextrous" organization, in which each activity has a separate budget, personnel, processes, and metrics for success. This approach allows the traditional organization to continue to pursue the profit-generating activities that sustain the current success of the business, and provides a protected environment for the innovators to take risks and explore new and disruptive approaches.[19]

In addition to creating a separate structure, these efforts have little chance of success without the personal attention and active oversight of the top leadership—in particular, the CEO. Bob Rivers clearly showed this commitment, providing significant time, attention, and financial resources to Eastern Labs. Developing senior team buy-in is also critical and requires a narrative and logic about the identity of the company that is broad enough to encompass the innovation activity. In addition, incentives, culture, and metrics, particularly compensation and bonus plans, must be modified to support the new goals across the entire senior team.

The most challenging aspect of ambidexterity is that, after innovations have been incubated in a separate, protected environment, they need to be successfully integrated back into the organization. This is an easier process if the benefits of the innovation are a two-way street. Rather than something that is done "over there," there must be aspects of the innovation that create immediate value to the traditional organization. For example, in Eastern Bank, loan officers began to realize that the new automated loan process was creating a better experience for their customers. Both loan officers and small business owners could get an answer more quickly, and the underwriting was generally aligned with the bank's own standards, making the process more efficient for everyone. In this process, they were also outmaneuvering their competition, by making sure that every creditworthy borrower who walked in the door or logged onto their website had a good experience and received a loan from Eastern. Rather than being a threat to the employees in the core business, technology was an opportunity to enable their success.

On the other hand, getting the whole organization behind an innovative idea can be hard to accomplish. The founder and former Chairman of Intuit, Scott Cook, a successful entrepreneur and sponsor of innovation, learned this lesson during an attempt to integrate a new tax product into his established business. While the innovation was valuable to the company, those in the traditional TurboTax business felt threatened by the new product and did not allow it to flourish. Eventually, despite a strong senior level commitment, the innovation died.[20]

Even with a commitment to innovation at the top, how does a traditional bank attract the talent necessary to transform the business? Some large banks have tried to create more entrepreneurial environments, such as Barclays with its "Rise" centers. In 2015, the Dutch banking group ING completely restructured the organization and operations of its Netherlands office, transitioning to an "agile" model inspired by that of large tech companies. In this way, they hoped to attract and retain innovation talent and compete as a fintech platform.[21] At Eastern, even though they ended up losing the initial team of innovators in the spin out, the CFO of the bank noted that Eastern Labs increased their reputational capital within the entrepreneurial community, making it easier to recruit new talent. As he put it, "We certainly got a lot of publicity and cache out of it. When I'm recruiting prospective hires, I'm always surprised at how interested they are in Labs."[22]

The Bank of the Future

What is the successful model for the small business bank of the future? Can today's banks evolve to be those players, or will they be beaten out by new entrants, small or large? There are three major hurdles that the banking industry must overcome to be successful in the new technology-enabled financial services environment. First, banks of the future will need a threshold level of data integration to provide the intelligence and customer service that small business lending will require. Small businesses will want to use their bank accounts, credit facilities, investment accounts, and other services in a much more seamless fashion. And from the bank's perspective, all of this information will be important for credit analysis. To do this, banks will need to find ways to evolve their legacy systems, whether they develop new technology in-house or provide integration with applications developed by third parties.

As we discussed in Chapter 8, the future will likely still involve relationships. The second hurdle is that the role of loan officers, those who interact with customers, can and should evolve, which means change for this key group of employees. Bankers will need to be trained to integrate their advice with the next generation of financial technology, in which small businesses will have more information to begin the conversation, and the loan officer's role will be to provide expertise and advice that supplements that information. In medicine, patients now have online access to their test results and WebMD, but only doctors have the expertise and training to interpret the data effectively and recommend a course of action. Likewise, loan officers of the future will need to serve as experts—working with small businesses who have more access to financial data on their business, but are unsure of how to interpret and use the information.

Finally, banks are not to be counted out of the ranks of the winners in the future world of small business lending, but to be successful, they will need to make clear decisions about what small business customers they wish to serve, and invest in new technology and tools to serve that segment's needs. The new world of technological solutions has increased small businesses' expectations from their banks, and that trend will only continue. Those banks that concentrate on small businesses and prioritize their needs will likely be the most successful in the new small business lending environment.

Part III

The Role of Regulation

10

Regulatory Obstacles: Confusion, Omission, and Overlap

In the mid-1960s, banks began to realize that a relatively recent innovation—credit cards—could become the next big contributor to their bottom lines. The first card that was usable at multiple merchants, Diners Club, was issued in 1950. This spurred financial firms to work out how to make offering them profitable and attractive enough to be adopted *en masse* by consumers and merchants. Among other improvements, they developed cards that could be used at any merchant— not just restaurants—anywhere in the country, and experimented with how to sign up more customers.[1]

By 1966, a group of Chicago banks thought they were ready to jump into the market with both feet. Just before that year's holiday season, these banks began to mail millions of unsolicited credit cards to Chicago residents, especially targeting affluent suburbanites. The effort turned out to be a disaster.

The banks' mailing lists were full of errors. Cards were sent to children, pets, and dead people. And since the banks publicized their effort, criminals were enticed to steal the cards, which did not require customers to activate them, from mailboxes and post offices. Some merchants even conspired with thieves to put banks on the hook to pay for fraudulent charges. In all, the Chicago Debacle led to an estimated $6 million to $12 million in losses.[2]

The scandal also produced scrutiny from legislators and reformers who realized that the financial regulatory system had not been adapted to handle the new cards. Some called for credit cards to be banned, but lawmakers took a more measured approach. During the late 1960s and 1970s, Congress passed several major consumer protection laws that banned a variety of abusive and predatory practices, and empowered consumers to dispute billing errors. In 1978, a Supreme Court ruling allowed banks to set credit card interest rates

© The Author(s) 2018
K. G. Mills, *Fintech, Small Business & the American Dream*,
https://doi.org/10.1007/978-3-030-03620-1_10

based on the home state of the bank, rather than having to abide by different interest rate caps in each state, which made broad credit card issuance more attractive to banks. Updated banking rules and regulations better protected consumers while creating more regulatory certainty for banks. As a result, the groundwork was laid for credit cards to become nearly ubiquitous in America.

In recent years, financial innovation has brought new lenders and loan products to the small business market that could have enormous potential. New actors, from fintech entrepreneurs, to nonbanks like Amazon and PayPal, are already operating under a legal and regulatory system that never anticipated their presence.

A hands-off approach to regulating online lending may result in more innovation, but innovations are not inherently good; they can be used by less scrupulous or predatory lenders to maximize their own profits at the expense of borrowers or the financial system. On the other hand, heavy-handed regulation may protect borrowers at the cost of a well-functioning market and the widespread development of affordable financial products and services for small businesses.

We need a balanced regulatory system that encourages innovation and helps small businesses find the best financing options for them, while simultaneously identifying and stopping the bad actors that can threaten the market. Unfortunately, the current financial regulatory system is flawed in ways that prevent the market from reaching this optimal state. Small businesses are paying for those flaws in the form of high costs, hidden charges, and confusing payment terms. And new innovation may be getting lost under the burden of overlapping, and sometimes overwhelming, rules and requirements.

Fintech Oversight Falls Through the Cracks of the Fragmented Regulatory System

No one would design the current U.S. financial regulatory system if they were to start from scratch. The existing structure was cobbled together piecemeal over more than 150 years, with Congress often responding to financial crises by creating at least one new federal financial regulatory agency. For example, in 1863, Congress created the Office of the Comptroller of the Currency (OCC) to help finance the Civil War and address inconsistencies in banking regulations among the states. The legislation that created the Federal Reserve (Fed) grew from the Panic of 1907, while the Great Depression led Congress to establish the Federal Deposit Insurance Corporation (FDIC) to prevent runs on bank deposits and the Securities and Exchange Commission (SEC) to provide oversight of securities markets. The creation of the Office of Thrift Supervision (OTS) was a response to the savings and loan crisis of the 1980s.

Following the 2008 financial crisis, Congress eliminated the OTS, which had failed to adequately supervise several large financial firms that were at the heart of the crisis, including American International Group, Inc. (AIG), Countrywide, and Washington Mutual. However, through the Dodd-Frank Act of 2010, Congress also created three new entities: the Consumer Financial Protection Bureau (CFPB), the Office of Financial Research (OFR), and the Financial Stability Oversight Council (FSOC). The result is not a model of efficiency or effectiveness. The U.S. financial regulatory system is fragmented, featuring multiple agencies—both state and federal—with overlapping jurisdictions engaged at times in duplicative, and even conflicting, activities.

Banks, thrifts (also known as savings and loans), and credit unions can all take customer deposits, but they are governed by different rules, and each can be chartered at the state or federal level. Each state has different rules for the depository institutions that it charters, while four different agencies—the Fed, the FDIC, the OCC, and the National Credit Union Administration (NCUA)—oversee federally chartered depositories and also have some authority to oversee state-chartered depositories. Collectively, these agencies are sometimes called "prudential" regulators, because their primary mission is to ensure the safety and soundness of the individual financial firms they oversee. Other financial regulatory agencies focus on oversight of certain activities rather than on individual firms. For example, the CFPB writes and enforces rules aimed at protecting consumers from predatory financial products. The SEC regulates securities activities with rules for trading, broker licensing, and transparency.

Few disagree that the financial regulatory structure is problematic. According to a recent report by the Government Accountability Office (GAO), the current regulatory structure, despite some strengths, "has created challenges to effective oversight. Fragmentation and overlap have created inefficiencies in regulatory processes, inconsistencies in how regulators oversee similar types of institutions, and differences in the levels of protection afforded to consumers. GAO has long reported on these effects in multiple areas of the regulatory system."[3] Figure 10.1 depicts the current U.S. regulatory structure which resembles a "spaghetti soup"—a tangle of interconnected entities, relationships, and rules.

The problems of fragmentation, overlap, and duplication never seem to get solved, but not for lack of ideas. Researchers from the Volcker Alliance catalogued no fewer than 45 legislative and official proposals to restructure the financial regulatory system between 1915 and 2013.[4] This does not include many of the proposals made by think tanks and other policymakers during the same period.

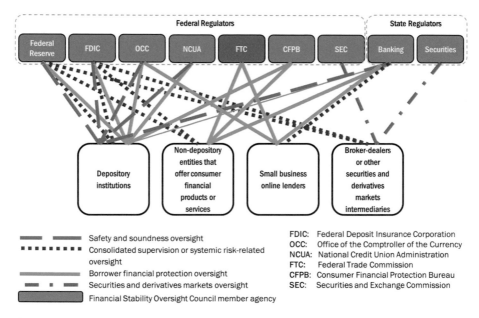

Figure 10.1   Small Business Online Lending Falls Through the Regulatory Cracks
Source: Adapted from GAO-16-175, "Financial Regulation: Complex and Fragmented Structure Could Be Streamlined to Improve Effectiveness," February 2016.

There are several reasons for the lack of reform. Opponents of reform have, over the years, argued that competition among regulatory agencies improves the overall quality of regulation and avoids overregulation, that reform will create uncertainty, or that the system works fine as it is. Regulators themselves may lobby to protect their jurisdictional "turf," and so too might members of congressional committees who would lose oversight authority over an agency within their jurisdiction if it were merged into another. Financial firms may also resist change because reform could mean extra costs of adjusting to a new supervisor and new rules.

Recent innovations in financial services have challenged regulators because new fintech firms are different entities than banks and other traditional financial institutions. Fintechs are subject to some of the same rules as other financial firms, to the extent that their activities are similar. But some of the regulatory regime either applies differently to fintechs, or does not apply to them at all. In fact, in its current state, small business lending has, in several important ways, fallen through the cracks of the current regulatory system. Specifically, until recently, there was no federal nonbank charter, and of even more concern, many of the protections consumers enjoy do not apply to small business borrowers.

Federal Agencies Did Not Charter Nonbank Lenders

There are at least seven federal agencies—not to mention states, each of which conducts its own banking and securities oversight—that have some regulatory authority over the banks and credit unions that lend to small businesses. But until 2018, none of these federal entities would grant charters to nonbank lenders, such as the new fintech competitors or nonbank platforms.

The Federal Reserve (Fed). The Fed oversees state-chartered banks and thrifts that are members of the Federal Reserve System, foreign bank organizations operating in the United States, and all holding companies that include banks or thrifts. The Fed has additional duties, including promoting the stability of the financial system, promoting consumer protection, and fostering a safe and efficient payment and settlement system.[5] The Fed also has a mandate to understand and monitor market conditions, including the small business lending market.

The Federal Deposit Insurance Corporation (FDIC). The FDIC provides deposit insurance and is the primary federal regulator for state-chartered banks that are not members of the Federal Reserve System.[6]

The Office of the Comptroller of the Currency (OCC). As an independent bureau of the U.S. Department of the Treasury, the OCC oversees all national banks, federal thrifts, and federal branches and agencies of foreign banks.[7] The OCC announced in 2018 that it would allow nonbanks to apply for a limited purpose bank charter, though some have challenged that the OCC has the authority to do so.

National Credit Union Administration (NCUA). The NCUA regulates and supervises federal credit unions, and insures the deposits of all federal and most state credit unions.

The Federal Trade Commission (FTC). The FTC was created in 1913 to prevent unfair competition and business practices that affect commerce generally, including lending to consumers and small businesses. The FTC adopted the Credit Practices Rule to protect consumers against abusive terms and conditions in credit contracts. In 2016, the FTC indicated that it intended to extend the same protections that consumers have in traditional lending to marketplace lending.[8]

The Consumer Financial Protection Bureau (CFPB). In the Dodd-Frank Act, Congress created the CFPB and gave it the mission to monitor consumer financial markets, including industries such as student loans, retail mortgages, and consumer credit cards. The CFPB has jurisdiction over a wide range of financial products and activities to ensure that the marketplace works for both lenders and borrowers, but only consumer borrowers.[9]

The Securities and Exchange Commission (SEC). The SEC protects investors in public markets, including publicly traded small business loan securities. The agency also supervises securitization markets and new securities, such as funds that invest in peer-to-peer loans.

Despite some of the gaps in direct authority, several federal agencies kept an eye on a portion of early fintech activities. Regional Federal Reserve banks included fintech questions in their coordinated credit surveys on small business lending. The SEC monitored the activities of online lenders that were raising capital in securities markets, paying special attention to protecting investors in those markets and ensuring that appropriate disclosures were made. State-level regulators granted charters and licenses to fintechs in their states. Yet, until the OCC stepped up to the task, the federal regulatory system did not have a central mechanism to oversee nonbank small business lenders.

Benefits of a Federal Charter Overseeing Nonbank Lenders

Most early online small business lenders were governed by a patchwork of state-by-state oversight that made compliance expensive, complicated, and time-consuming. Nonbank lenders essentially had two options: (1) lending directly to borrowers by acquiring licenses and being supervised in each state in which they operated, or (2) originating loans through a partnership with a national or state bank. Some new entrants specifically designed their products so they did not qualify as loans, to avoid regulation and regulatory uncertainties.

The tangle of multi-state oversight raises compliance costs, especially for new and small firms. Large companies are better able than small or start-up firms to absorb these costs, which could cause start-ups to wait until regulation becomes more certain, thus stifling innovation.[10] To their credit, state regulators recognized these issues, and the Conference of State Bank Supervisors (CSBS) began efforts to coordinate and align regulation across states. In 2018, they issued an ambitious plan to adopt an "integrated, 50-state licensing and supervisory system, leveraging technology and smart regulatory policy" by 2020.[11] The initiative is admirable, but will probably take more time than projected and will likely encounter resistance, so it may not be the ultimate answer.

In 2016, the OCC announced that it would allow nonbanks to apply for a special purpose federal bank charter. Under the category of "no good deed goes unpunished," this proposal was met with objections from multiple parties, including existing fintechs that had already gone through the pain of registering in every state and did not want to see new competitors find an easier path. Banks thought the charter would be "banking light" and disadvantage them. The state bank supervisors went so far as to file a complaint against the OCC proposal in U.S. District Court.

In July 2018, the OCC went forward with a charter that would allow nonbank lenders to become special purpose national banks. In its announcement of the move, the OCC affirmed support for federal regulation of innovative fintech firms saying, "The federal banking system must continue to evolve and embrace innovation to meet the changing customer needs and serve as a source of strength for the nation's economy. The decision to consider applications for special purpose national bank charters from innovative companies helps provide more choices to consumers and businesses, and creates greater opportunity for companies that want to provide banking services in America. Companies that provide banking services in innovative ways deserve the opportunity to pursue that business on a national scale as a federally chartered, regulated bank."[12]

This was a good step forward. With a national charter, online and other nonbank small business lenders will be able to operate nationwide, subject to a consistent set of federal standards that will increase transparency and benefit small businesses. The lenders will have a single supervisor and examination process, which should reduce barriers to entry and lower costs. Small business borrowers should benefit from these lower costs and additional innovation in new products and services from new nonbank providers.

Lack of Coordinated Third-Party Regulation Discourages Innovation

There are also regulatory frictions facing banks that want to partner with fintechs to bring innovative lending options to their small business customers. These partnerships fall under the category of "third-party arrangements" and are subject to oversight from a number of entities.

In 2013, the OCC issued guidance for banks on how to manage risks that may arise from their relationships with third parties, such as brokers, payments processors, and IT vendors. The OCC said that it would expect banks to use "more comprehensive and rigorous oversight" of third-party relationships that involved "critical activities." The OCC set out an eight-phase process for managing risk with third parties, including due diligence, ongoing monitoring, documentation and reporting, and independent reviews.[13] In 2017, in response to questions from banks, the OCC clarified that fintech firms are also subject to the 2013 guidance.[14]

It is difficult to fault the OCC for wanting to better understand the risk that third parties might pose to the safety and soundness of banks that they supervise. However, the OCC is not the only agency interested in third-party risk. A national bank would be supervised by the OCC, but its holding company would be overseen by the Fed, and the FDIC would have an interest as well since it manages the Deposit Insurance Fund that guarantees the bank's deposits.[15] The CFPB would also supervise the bank's activities.

It would make sense for these agencies to coordinate on their expectations for third-party risk management, but that has not always been the case. The result has been overlapping and duplicative requirements that make partnerships between banks and fintechs difficult and time-consuming. In July 2018, the U.S. Department of the Treasury (Treasury) recognized these issues and asked federal regulators to review and harmonize their third-party guidance. Treasury also focused on clarifying when data aggregators are subject to third-party guidance, an issue important to the use of APIs.[16] This sets the right direction, although this kind of coordination between federal regulators is easier said than done.

The Current Regulatory System Is Not Well-Designed to Identify and Thwart Bad Actors

One of the most worrisome issues with the current regulatory system is that the new consumer protections put into place after the 2008 financial crisis do not apply to small businesses. These protections are restricted to consumers, largely because small business owners have historically been viewed as sophisticated enough to fend for themselves in lending markets. This means that many rules, including those related to providing borrowers with standardized and understandable information about the terms of their loans (such as annual percentage rate—APR—and repayment terms), are not required for small business or other commercial loans.

Consumer Lending Protections Don't Apply to Small Businesses

In 2015, the Fed interviewed a group of "mom & pop" small businesses about lending options. The 44 participating businesses had between 2 and 20 employees and less than $2 million in annual revenues, representing a variety of industries and regions of the United States.[17] The owners were asked to compare several sample loan products, as shown in Figure 10.2.

They were then asked to answer the following question: "What is your 'best guess' of the interest rate on product A?" (Figure 10.3).

The participants' answers were all over the map, ranging from 5 percent to over 50 percent. In reality, it is a trick question. The interest rate on Option A cannot be calculated with the information provided because the effective rate would vary depending on how long it took for the borrower to pay back the loan. But many small business owners in the focus groups had answers they perceived to be correct.

From 2015 to 2017, we presented this same exercise to several groups of students and alumni at Harvard Business School and got a similar range of answers. The truth is, even with a financially sophisticated audience, the costs on a relatively simple small business loan can be difficult to understand and compare. The Fed conducted another set of focus groups in 2017, presenting small business owners with financing and loan descriptions similar to those on online lending sites. Again, they saw that small business owners found the descriptions of the loans confusing.[18]

Figure 2	Product A	Product B	Product C
Amount borrowed	$40,000	$40,000	$40,000
Information you provide	Your sales history and bank account information, tax returns, etc. You send the information directly to the lender through mail or email.	You give permission to have your records pulled electronically for your sales history, bank accounts, inventory, and online reviews of your business.	Your bank account information, tax returns, and three years of financial statements. You send the information directly to the lender through mail or email. You pledge collateral to secure the loan.
Credit score	You need at least a 500 FICO	You need at least a 650 FICO	You need at least a 700 FICO
Waiting period for decision	3 to 5 days	2 hours	7 days
How soon funds arrive in your account	3 to 5 business days after you are approved	The same day you are approved	4 weeks
Repayment information provided	You owe $52,000. The company takes 10 percent of your debit/credit card sales receipts each day until it is paid off.	You owe the original $40,000 plus 28 cents for every dollar you borrow. The loan is paid off in one year.	You owe monthly payments of $3,440. Your effective APR is 6.0%. The loan is paid off in one year.

Figure 10.2   Loan Options Presented to Small Business Owners—2015
Cleveland Fed Focus Groups and borrower interviews
Source: Barbara J. Lipman and Ann Marie Wiersch, "Alternative Lending through the Eyes of 'Mom & Pop' Small-Business Owners: Findings from Online Focus Groups," Federal Reserve Bank of Cleveland, August 25, 2015.

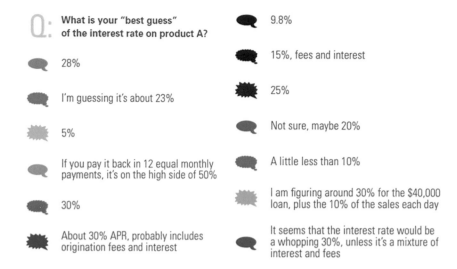

Figure 10.3   Borrowers Had Trouble Understanding Loan Terms
Small business owners' guesses of APR on product A
Source: Barbara J. Lipman and Ann Marie Wiersch, "Alternative Lending through the Eyes of 'Mom & Pop' Small-Business Owners: Findings from Online Focus Groups," Federal Reserve Bank of Cleveland, August 25, 2015.

Nearly all of the small business owners in the 2017 Fed focus groups said they wanted clear, easy-to-understand disclosures about all costs, payment policies, and potential penalties to help them make informed decisions and compare credit offerings. And why shouldn't they? Such disclosures are helpful in making decisions and are required for consumer, mortgage, and student loans, so why not for small business loans?

Small businesses should be empowered not only to make better credit decisions, but also to protect themselves from predatory and otherwise unscrupulous lenders. Several problems have already emerged in the online lending market, which have caused concern among regulators, policymakers, consumer protection advocates, and responsible lenders. Some of these practices parallel the "four Ds" of predation—deception, debt traps, debt spirals, and discrimination—that former CFPB Director Richard Cordray sought to end in other sectors, such as mortgage, student, and payday consumer loans.

Emerging Issues in Small Business Lending

The most worrisome emerging issues relate to high loan costs and terms that may not be fully disclosed and can make the loan difficult to sustain and repay.

High Costs

There are many ways to evaluate the cost of credit. A borrower can calculate the daily and monthly repayment, financing charges, origination and other up-front fees, the total cost of capital, the interest rate, and the APR of a loan. APR, which measures the interest rate a borrower would pay for credit in a year, is not a perfect metric, but it has become the standard in consumer lending. The APRs of some newer financing products can run well above 50 percent and can reach more than 100 percent.[19,20] Although lenders often argue that disclosing APRs does not paint the full picture—and for short-term credit they can be correct—some of these prices are high enough that one wonders how a small business can sustain the loan.

Inadequate or Nonexistent Disclosure of Price and Terms

Borrowers may not even know they are paying high prices because, as we have discussed earlier, disclosures that are required for consumer, student, and mortgage loans do not apply to small business loans. While some responsible lenders have chosen to provide extensive and transparent disclosures, others might disclose the information differently, or not at all. The result is that borrowers don't have access to clear metrics they can use to shop and compare loans across products and lenders, as they do with consumer loans or auto insurance.

Double Dipping and Debt Traps

Small business owners who borrow short-term credit that they fail to repay are often forced to roll over their debt into another loan, which piles additional fees onto the underlying loan. Rollovers can easily turn into a debt trap in which credit ends up becoming difficult to escape.[21] One practice that creates this trap for the small business owner is known as "double dipping," in which a lender charges a borrower additional fees when their loan is renewed, before the term of the original outstanding loan is complete.

Confusion Over Prepayment Costs

Unlike traditional term loans that amortize over time, the financing charges of some newer short-term products are fixed, meaning that if borrowers repay early, charges are still incurred for the full term of the loan. In the 2017 Fed focus groups, these loans confused many borrowers who thought that paying early would save them interest.[22]

Misaligned Broker Incentives

Small business loan brokers earn higher referral fees for more expensive products. It can also be difficult for borrowers to understand the costs a broker adds to their loan. Moreover, the lack of disclosure prevents a borrower from understanding when a broker may have incentives that conflict with the best interests of the borrower.

Misaligned incentives can cause major problems, as we saw prior to the 2008 financial crisis, when many mortgage brokers were paid based on the number of mortgages they originated, often with little attention to whether the borrower was able or likely to repay the loan. Borrowers in the Fed focus groups expressed concerns about being bombarded with solicitations by companies and brokers after doing a search for online financing. Discussing the issue of brokers in fintech, the former chief executive officer of Opportunity Finance Network—a trade association of Community Development Financial Institutions (CDFIs)—said, "It's a direct parallel to what happened in the subprime mortgage space."[23]

Policymakers Lack Data on Small Business Lending and Fintech Activity

One overarching issue facing regulators and small business advocates is that it is not clear how pervasive predatory activities and high costs are in the small business lending market. This is because there is no comprehensive data on real-time loan originations and pricing for small business lending. The lack of data leads to the worst of both worlds: legislators and regulators without fact-based analysis are left to respond to anecdotal stories of small businesses that have been taken advantage of by bad actors, and well-meaning lenders are left confused and concerned about how unclear rules will be implemented.

The sources now available—FDIC call report data on commercial and industrial (C&I) lending, Fed surveys, and private sources—are all rough proxies for small business lending. There is no systematic data collection on a host of important areas, such as loan applications and approvals, and the ability of different demographic groups to acquire credit. And there is no information on the costs of the loans. All of this makes it difficult to adequately assess, particularly in real time, the dynamics of the small business lending market and to develop sound policy around it.

Imagine being a member of Congress during the next recession and wondering how you should act on reports of small businesses shuttering their doors around the country and in your home state. It would be hard to respond effectively without good data. And yet, that is the position in which U.S. policymakers have long placed themselves.

A partial solution to this data collection issue was included in Section 1071 of the Dodd-Frank Act, which was passed in 2010. The provision requires the CFPB to gather and review certain data on small business lending. This includes collecting data on loan originations and on fair lending practices, with a particular goal of ensuring that women and minority-owned small businesses receive equitable access to credit. An initial statement from the CFPB indicated that it would act "expeditiously" to develop these rules, but the Bureau focused first on its consumer regulations and fell behind.[24] It was not until 2017 that an official request for information was released to help formulate the rules, and little additional progress was made in 2018.[25]

Section 1071 has also encountered strong resistance from many banks and others concerned about the increased cost burden of collecting the required data. The anticipated difficulties stem from the fact that there is no universal definition of a small business, and that the information required to determine size and ownership is either not collected on applications, or not collected in uniform or reliable ways. Banks and others are also worried that the information will be used after the fact to show bias in lending patterns that was unknown or unintended.

Some of these concerns are understandable. But the answer cannot be to simply do nothing and allow policymakers and regulators to "fly blind" when it comes to small business lending. One proposed solution is to start with data that is available, such as loan originations by loan size, which are currently known by banks and relatively straightforward to report, and if collected could provide enormously valuable information on small business lending markets. In fact, a 2018 Bipartisan Policy Center Task Force on Main Street Finance Report recommended that the OFR collect and store the relevant data and work with the Small Business Administration's (SBA's) Office of Advocacy to publish reports and analysis.[26] Another approach would be to have a confidential third party, such as a university, collect and hold the data and make it available to academics, policymakers, and legislators on an aggregated basis for analysis and rulemaking. Solutions can be found for the concerns around data collection, and more granular information will undoubtedly improve the ability of both regulators and the market to meet the needs of small business borrowers.

*   *   *

There is something to be said for light-touch regulation, which can stimulate innovation and benefit borrowers as well as lenders. Since online lenders have had to comply with fewer rules, they have experimented with more creative, automated underwriting techniques that allow them to make faster lending decisions. They have made the credit application experience friendlier by taking advantage of the seamless user interfaces that have become common to online companies. And they have extended credit to a broader range of borrowers than traditional lenders.

But as the Chicago Debacle of 1966 illustrates, limited regulatory oversight has drawbacks too. In the case of online lending, too many lenders have failed to disclose adequate information about prices and terms.[27,28] Federal regulators provide little oversight of online small business lending, specifically in regards to borrower protections for small businesses seeking capital, which has created many concerns about predatory lending.

A well-functioning financial regulatory system will help ensure that responsible lenders can compete and expand access to capital for qualified borrowers. Responsible regulation needs to protect borrowers and investors, and mitigate systemic risk, while at the same time promoting innovation. It can be a tricky balance to strike, but it is a balance that is necessary to improve the state of small business lending. In Chapter 11, we suggest some principles for financial services reform that should guide the small business lending regulatory system of the future.

11

The Regulatory System of the Future

Fintech innovations will alter the financial system. In the small business lending segment, there will be new lenders and new products and services, many of which will use data in ways that have never before been contemplated. The ownership, security, and use—or misuse—of data will be defining issues in this coming era. Regulatory challenges will accelerate as technology influences more and more parts of the banking and payments industries. We cannot predict the future exactly, but we can be proactive and reform our financial regulatory system to better prepare for the kinds of changes that are coming.

We propose three core principles for how to approach reform and shape future governance. The first principle is to promote innovation by creating an environment that encourages new approaches, and does not allow risk aversion to stifle the potential for exciting and valuable small business products and services to emerge from this fintech revolution. At the same time, there must be guiderails and protections, both for the borrowers and for the financial system as a whole. So the second principle is to protect small businesses, both from "bad actors" we can identify today and also from risks stemming from the new use of data and artificial intelligence. Third, the U.S. regulatory system needs to undergo a streamlining process that will allow it to function more effectively and continue to promote an environment where U.S. financial service firms can be world leaders. These principles draw on lessons from other countries, particularly the United Kingdom and China, and build on industry self-regulation proposals made by some early actors in fintech.

© The Author(s) 2018
K. G. Mills, *Fintech, Small Business & the American Dream*,
https://doi.org/10.1007/978-3-030-03620-1_11

Industry Efforts to Self-Regulate

As hundreds of new fintech players entered the market, many of the first movers in the industry were aware of problems emerging in online small business lending and took steps to self-regulate. The objective was to weed out bad actors and avoid a "race to the bottom" characterized by low transparency and high pricing that could result in responsible players being shut out of the market. The industry also hoped to avoid more stringent government regulation through effective self-regulation.

One of these efforts, the Small Business Borrowers' Bill of Rights, was developed in 2015 and updated in 2017 by online lenders such as Lending Club and Fundera, and by non-industry stakeholders such as the Small Business Majority, the Aspen Institute, and the National League of Cities.[1] The Small Business Borrowers' Bill of Rights proposed six "fundamental financing rights" to which the signatories believed small business borrowers were entitled, including the right to transparent pricing and terms, non-abusive products, responsible underwriting, fair treatment from brokers, inclusive credit access, and fair collection practices.[2]

We believe that these are the right kinds of principles for the industry to adopt, and the Small Business Borrowers' Bill of Rights remains a worthy template. However, it is only a template, not a detailed guide for implementing regulation. For example, no specific format has been agreed upon for the practice of providing borrowers with information that is easily comparable across loan products, although several groups have proposed solutions. One model was the single-page disclosures for mortgage lenders required by the Consumer Financial Protection Bureau (CFPB). Another suggested format called the SMART Box—developed by an industry group led by OnDeck, Lendio, PayNet, and Kabbage—included the loan and repayment amounts, the cost of capital broken out in detail, interest rate (annual percentage rate—APR), and the term of the loan, on a single page.[3]

Self-regulation can be effective. For example, the American Bar Association (ABA) developed Model Rules of Professional Conduct to set minimum standards for attorneys to follow. Many states adopted all or part of these standards into their own legally binding rules for ethics and conduct. Although the online lending industry came up with some strong proposals, they have not been widely adopted even among those who suggested them. The self-regulation effort would benefit from greater coordination, more commitment among lenders to participate, and a way to raise the consequences for lenders that do not comply.

Unfortunately, it is likely the case that self-policing and voluntary disclosures alone will not stop predatory lenders, since principles and best practices do not have the force of law. Only regulation can compel every lender and broker to treat borrowers fairly. Without universal standards, it is more difficult for lenders and brokers to abide by high standards when they have competitors that behave less ethically. Thus, it falls to policymakers to create a legal structure that rewards good industry behavior for fintechs, as they have for banks.

Lessons from Other Countries

America is not the only nation facing these questions. Since fintech innovation is a global phenomenon, there are already lessons—good and bad—that U.S. policymakers can learn from the experiences of foreign regulators.

Positive Lessons from the United Kingdom

During the 2008 financial crisis, former U.K. Chancellor of the Exchequer, George Osborne, recalled being flooded with calls to help small businesses get access to credit.[4] The crisis and recession hit the United Kingdom's small and medium-sized enterprises (SMEs) hard. Osborne and then Prime Minister David Cameron soon realized that the government had few tools available to address SME lending and thereby help stabilize the economy. Unlike the United States, which had a network of more than 5,000 community banks, over 80 percent of U.K. SME lending was done by four large banks, and all four were in trouble.

The crisis triggered aggressive steps by the U.K. government to help SME lending recover. There are several lessons from that effort, which the United States could do well to learn. These fall into five categories: (1) the benefits of creating a single oversight agency with a mandate to protect the financial system and encourage competition; (2) the need to create mechanisms in the regulatory environment that encourage and support innovation; (3) the adoption of a systematic review of the new rules that regulate new entities in order to make sure they are working properly; (4) the value of collecting data that allows policymakers to monitor the levels of and gaps in small business lending; and (5) that markets will be more innovative and more secure if consumers and small businesses control their own data.

The Financial Conduct Authority

In 2013, the British government created a new agency, the Financial Conduct Authority (FCA), to supervise the business conduct of more than 56,000 financial services firms to make sure that financial markets were "honest, fair, and effective." It also became the prudential regulator for about 18,000 firms, charged with ensuring their safety and soundness.[5]

But unlike most regulators, the FCA was given a third strategic objective: to promote "effective competition in the interest of consumers." This competition mandate allowed the FCA to take on a proactive agenda around fintech and innovation, in a way few regulators had ever envisioned. The approach led to the creation of Project Innovate, a much-discussed program for innovative fintech firms to try out some of their business ideas before taking them to the broader market. Perhaps the most interesting aspect of this initiative was the Regulatory Sandbox, a place for businesses to test innovative products, services, business models, and delivery mechanisms in a live environment without immediately incurring all the normal regulatory consequences of engaging in the activity in question."[6]

For example, say a start-up has a new algorithm that might better predict the creditworthiness of potential borrowers. Once the firm was in the sandbox, they received individualized regulatory guidance from the FCA staff, became eligible to receive waivers or modifications of existing FCA rules, and could apply for "no enforcement action" letters that limited disciplinary action if the firm dealt openly with the FCA.[7,8] All of these activities were designed to help start-ups test new ideas while simultaneously allowing the FCA to monitor industry developments. In the first year the sandbox was in operation, the FCA received 146 applications for its first two six-month cohorts, and accepted 50 of those into the program.[9]

Routine Reviews of Regulatory Effectiveness

In 2010, in response to the financial crisis, Her Majesty's (HM) Treasury implemented a series of regulations that provided an oversight structure for fintechs involved in the U.K. peer-to-peer lending markets, which were growing rapidly. The regulations were enacted quickly, in less than nine months. Because the markets were new, HM Treasury officials built in an additional provision—the entire set of rules would be reviewed in one to two years to be sure they were working. This idea of quickly implementing, then reviewing and adapting legislation, is absent from U.S. lawmaking and may be hard to effect, but the concept would be useful as fintech regulation will need to evolve as products and markets respond to new innovations.

Mandated Industry Data Collection

The United Kingdom also took aggressive actions post-crisis on the data collection front. The newly created British Business Bank (BBB) became responsible for gathering quarterly data from banks and online lenders on loan originations and loan stocks, including metrics on costs and defaults, to better track the availability of credit and the progress of market reforms. The BBB focused particularly on the SME lending market and on the fintech marketplace in general. Further, banks were required to share commercial loan data in confidential formats with regulators and policymakers, and make this information available to competitors via credit agencies to improve credit assessments and oversight of potential discrimination. This effort appeared to be valuable for policymaking and monitoring of the market's recovery.

Data Ownership—PSD2 and Open Banking

In 2018, a landmark set of regulations governing financial data took effect in Europe. The Revised Payments Services Directive (PSD2) upended the status quo in the financial system by giving customers explicit ownership of their financial data and requiring banks to share this data with third-party service providers through open application programming interfaces (APIs) at a customer's request.[10] PSD2 allowed third parties to more easily aggregate and analyze data from multiple sources and present it in a seamless way. It also leveled the playing field between banks and fintechs, since incumbent firms were not allowed to monopolize customer data. PSD2 included a number of other provisions, including efforts to better safeguard the privacy of data. The United Kingdom implemented its own version of PSD2, called Open Banking, which, in addition to requiring that banks share data with third-party providers, required banks to provide that data in a standardized format.[11]

Although the long-term impacts of PSD2 and Open Banking have yet to play out, they frame a critical question for U.S. policymakers: the ownership of data. Having small businesses own their financial data and be the decision makers about who gets access to it, changes the competitive dynamics of the market. Under this regulatory framework, new financial services provider would have an equal opportunity to gain access to the information and create novel small business products and applications. The new regulations will be closely watched to see if PSD2 and Open Banking make markets more competitive and innovative than if banks control their customers' data.

Cautionary Tales from China

The regulation of alternative lending in China started out with a light touch approach, with the benefits and consequences one might expect. In China, peer-to-peer lending had a long history, with people lending directly to friends and relatives, and indirectly through rotating credit and savings associations.[12] Online platform lenders built on this tradition and flourished, with rapid growth in the number of platforms. The Chinese government encouraged innovation in the sector starting in 2013.[13] By 2015, peer-to-peer trading volume in China was four times what it was in the United States.[14] In that year, an average of three new lending platforms were coming online each day, and the volume of loans was growing by hundreds of percent annually.

Online lending proved particularly important for Chinese small businesses, which have long found it difficult to secure financing from traditional banks that are often at least partially controlled by the state. Even though SMEs account for 60 percent of the Chinese GDP and 80 percent of its urban employment, they receive only 20 to 25 percent of bank loans and are often forced to pay APRs of up to 60 percent for credit.[15]

Despite the fact that the Chinese financial regulatory system has been known as being heavy-handed and conservative in general, oversight of peer-to-peer lending was almost nonexistent until 2016. With no formal disclosure guidelines or regulation from national regulators, problems arose. As the number of online platforms mushroomed, so did the share that had been investigated by the police and those where the owners had walked away with investor funds or where loan repayments had ceased (Figure 11.1). The 2016 Blue Book of Internet Finance backed up this assessment, finding that more than one-third of Chinese platforms either had cases of fraud, or had gone or were going out of business.[16]

In December 2015, authorities shut down Ezubao, an online peer-to-peer broker that turned out to be a giant Ponzi scheme that collapsed after collecting about $9 billion from more than 900,000 investors.[17] Ezubao had promised some investors returns of nearly 15 percent per year, much higher than banks were offering. But one senior manager at the firm later said that "95 percent of investment projects on Ezubao were fake." Near the end, police had to resort to digging up 80 travel bags full of financial documents buried six feet underground by company officials.[18] Ezubao helped spark a government crackdown on numerous problems in China's peer-to-peer lending market.

In 2016, the Chinese government announced a series of new guidelines and rules. They defined online lending, banned platforms from engaging in certain activities such as pooling lender funds or providing credit enhancement services, set registration rules for platforms, required that plat-

Platforms

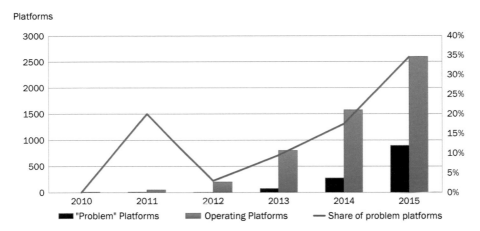

Figure 11.1   Number of Online Chinese Peer-to-Peer Platforms and Share of "Problem" Platforms
Source: Martin Chorzempa, "P2P Series Part 1: Peering Into China's Growing Peer-to-Peer Lending Market," Peterson Institute for International Economics, June 27, 2016.

forms use a qualified bank as a fund custodian, and set 65 mandatory and 31 encouraged disclosures.[19] The China Banking Regulatory Commission announced additional transparency rules in 2017, including that peer-to-peer platforms had to disclose funding sources, details about outstanding loans and repayment plans, and lending activity with people and companies connected to the platform.[20] Afterward, peer-to-peer loans continued to grow rapidly while the number of platforms fell by more than half between 2015 and 2018, indicating that the regulation may have had the desired impact of eliminating fraudulent players, but not stifling market growth.[21]

The Chinese market has also seen the rise of several large platform companies that have entered the small business lending space. In 2018, Ant Financial, the parent company for Alipay and an affiliate of ecommerce giant Alibaba, cemented itself as the largest fintech firm in the world by establishing a $150 billion valuation.[22] Ant and Alipay have become "the modern gateway to an ecosystem of financial services," not only dominating the mobile wallet and payments space, but also providing wealth management, insurance, credit scores, and consumer lending services.[23]

This growth has not gone unnoticed by the Chinese authorities, who have taken steps to limit Ant Financial's ambitions, such as curtailing its effort to create a national credit scoring system. The success of Ant has drawn the ire of China's traditional financial institutions, with one observer calling them "a vampire sucking blood from banks."[24] The banks have claimed that the company's practices decreased deposits, forcing higher interest rates and branch closures. We do not yet know whether the rise of dominant players in China's fintech market will be a positive or negative development for China's SMEs. But it is worth watching carefully as an example of how platform companies such as Amazon could become a powerful force in financial markets in the United States.

*   *   *

U.S. regulators can learn from the experiences of both China and the United Kingdom as they develop financial regulatory systems around the new fintech innovators. China's initial experience showed the dangers of too little oversight. Left alone, the bad actors already present in the U.S. market could accelerate their activities to the detriment of small businesses and the economy. The U.K. model, in contrast, provides useful guideposts, as the government and regulatory activities have been robust yet measured, straightforward yet comprehensive, and have produced real successes. The U.K. example demonstrates an effective balance of encouraging innovation and risk-taking with oversight and data collection. Despite the rigidity and polarization of American politics around regulatory reform, this model would not be difficult for U.S. regulators to emulate.

Principles for U.S. Financial Reform

For the good of America's small businesses, we must move on from the polarized view that any new financial regulation is bad for industry and consumers, as well as the opposing view that financial firms are untrustworthy, and must have ever-more rules piled upon them. In their 2003 book, *Saving Capitalism from the Capitalists*, Raghuram Rajan and Luigi Zingales make the argument that protecting free markets requires government intervention.[25] Governments need to guarantee property rights for the large and small alike to ensure that incumbents don't use their political advantage to benefit themselves, but also to provide a safety net for those who are the losers from economic displacement. The authors also suggest that too much government regulation of finance can actually benefit incumbents and insiders rather than encourage dynamic markets and benefit consumers and investors. Balance is the key.

Innovation has made its way into financial services, and the changes technology will bring to products and markets will continue. The entry of platforms and the more pervasive use of data and artificial intelligence are likely to impact lending markets dramatically. The Basel Committee on Banking Supervision summarized the moment: "fintech has the potential to lower barriers of entry to the financial services market and elevate the role of data as a key commodity, and drive the emergence of new business models. As a result, the scope and nature of banks' risks and activities are rapidly changing and rules governing them may need to evolve as well. These developments may indeed prove to be more disruptive than previous changes in the banking industry, although as with any forecast, this is in no way certain."[26] Change is coming, and our regulatory system is not yet prepared to meet these challenges.

Remaking the U.S. financial regulatory system will be difficult, but we should make our best attempt to be proactive. The answer is not more or less regulation, but the right regulation—balanced, sensible rules that operate in a transparent environment. It is time for an active agenda of financial regulatory reform in small business lending that is guided by three broad principles: (1) supporting innovation; (2) enhancing protections for small business borrowers while ensuring the safety of the financial system; and (3) streamlining and simplifying the regulatory environment.

Principle 1: Promote Innovation

Allowing small businesses to have a wider variety of financing choices will benefit lenders, small businesses, and the entire economy. There are several ways that the regulatory system can help to achieve this goal.

Engage with Innovators

The United Kingdom has provided a model for how regulators and fintech innovators can engage to encourage responsible innovation. The FCA's Regulatory Sandbox has given innovators a way to test their products and gain valuable feedback on how they should be designed to pass regulatory muster. This approach also helps regulators to understand changes in technology and methods, and how best to adapt to them. Many other countries have followed the United Kingdom's lead and created fintech sandboxes of their own, including Australia, Singapore, and China.[27]

In 2017, the Office of the Comptroller of the Currency (OCC) created a new Office of Innovation, which included a "light" version of a sandbox. The proposal offered tools for fintechs and others with new ideas to collaborate with regulators, but did not have the ability to waive legal liability for participants.[28] In another attempt, the Arizona State Legislature passed legislation in 2018 to create its own fintech sandbox, with other states considering taking similar action.[29]

These are a good start, but as the U.K. model demonstrates, regulators need to do more than pay lip service to innovation by saying they have a "sandbox." A real effort requires clear direction to fintech innovators about the rules of engagement: what are the protections afforded by the admission to the innovation environment? How long do these permissions last? What rules need to be followed in terms of disclosures? How do they apply to become active under the sandbox? Coordination among the state and federal regulators to allow firms to enter the sandbox will also be a necessary component, given how many entities have oversight.

Data Ownership, Privacy, and Transparency

Data is a key ingredient of many of the new innovations that will transform small business lending. This leads to a series of challenging questions facing not just financial services regulators, but multiple actors responsible for government oversight and protection. These issues are particularly acute when it comes to sensitive financial data. Policymakers will need to decide who owns different kinds of data, including transaction information, and a small business's credit score. Significant concerns arise around whether a business should have the right to know what is driving their credit score and what they can do to improve it.

Most small business advocates believe that more transparency is better, and that where possible, small businesses should own their own data. Innovators who have developed proprietary credit scoring or other algorithms, however, are concerned that too much transparency will undermine their competitive advantage and lead to less innovation. The right answer should be a balanced approach—with the weight on small business disclosure.

On the question of data ownership, many lessons can be taken from PSD2 and, in the United Kingdom, from the 2018 implementation of Open Banking. This new approach to data regulation has two key components: First, customers and small businesses own their data that resides in banks. Second, they can also release that data seamlessly through APIs to be used by other entities. The intent is to both protect data privacy and allow greater innovation in the use of data for the benefit of consumers and small businesses. Although the results are not yet known, U.S. regulators need to watch the European experience closely, and strongly consider whether a form of Open Banking framework would benefit the American market.

Principle 2: Look Out for Small Businesses

Current regulations need to be adjusted to make sure that small businesses have greater protections, particularly as new innovative products and services emerge in the market.

Require Appropriate Disclosures in Small Business Lending

If a person applies for a loan to buy a pickup truck for themselves, they are protected by numerous consumer laws and regulations, including standardized price and term disclosures. But if that same person applies for a loan to buy a pickup truck to expand their small lawn care business, many of those same protections do not apply. Given that small business borrowers are often hard to distinguish from consumer borrowers, this dichotomy makes little sense. And, at a more fundamental level, all borrowers should be able to easily understand and compare their credit options.

A 2007 Federal Trade Commission (FTC) study found that disclosures that enabled cross-comparisons dramatically increased borrowers' ability to understand mortgage options.[30] Loan disclosures already exist for consumers in formats that work, so lenders can begin by using these as examples. And as we have seen, small business owners want to be aware of the cost, fees, and terms of loans in order to make good credit decisions. Simply extending the Truth in Lending Act (TILA) provisions to small businesses might be the easiest solution.[31] However, given that consumer and small business loan products may have increasingly different characteristics, a more tailored set of protections will likely be required.[32]

Collect Small Business Lending Data

The first task for policymakers should be to improve the quality of data available on small business lending in a way that is minimally burdensome for regulators and financial firms. It is the critical step that will make every other action on small business policy easier. The most important data to collect is information about small business loan originations. This should include information on the type and purpose of the credit being applied for, the amount of credit applied for and provided (if any), whether the application was approved or denied, and demographic and location information on the applicant.

These metrics are already required by Dodd-Frank Section 1071. In Chapter 10, we suggested ways to phase in their collection, and mitigate industry concerns about implementation of the provision. Regulating complex financial markets is a demanding job. A lack of good data about the transactions in those markets raises the degree of difficulty in identifying and stopping bad actors, and in designing good small business policy.

Protect Small Businesses from Discrimination

With the influx of large of amounts of data in the underwriting process comes new responsibilities. As lenders increasingly rely on personal information and transaction data as part of their standardized algorithms, it will be imperative to adapt oversight to avoid adverse discriminatory effects. Our story in Chapter 8 about predicting a driver's accidents based on whether or not they buy frozen pizza may have seemed like an innocuous example. But, it fore-shadows real dangers about how artificial intelligence will be used and its potential to marginalize certain populations. These are not imaginary con-cerns—troubling examples of applied artificial intelligence are emerging in social media and other platforms, and financial services will not be far behind.

Building a smart oversight environment in a financial services world driven by big data will be complicated. Financial firms that use AI or other algo-rithms to guide how they engage with customers will need to share the inner workings of their models with regulatory agencies. Regulators will need the expertise to assess these complex activities, and the data to see if discrimina-tory outcomes are occurring. One useful parallel is the process that regulators have used to build expertise on how to oversee banks' internal risk models since the financial crisis. A priority for financial regulators should be to develop transparent and secure communication with lenders about the algorithms and machine learning tools they are using, and the outcomes from those algorithms on protected classes.

Principle 3: Streamline the Financial Regulatory System

The often-conflicting authorities of individual regulatory agencies make com-pliance needlessly difficult for industry participants. Even before online lend-ing came into the picture, many small banks expressed frustration and anxiety about conflicting directives received from different agencies about the same loan. In addition, each agency has its own examination process, which results in duplicative requests for information, and other inefficiencies.

Numerous proposals have been made over the years to reduce the fragmen-tation and overlap in the U.S. financial regulatory system. A 2014 report from the Bipartisan Policy Center recommended a comprehensive overhaul that would include consolidating the bank prudential regulatory functions of the Federal Reserve (Fed), the Federal Deposit Insurance Corporation (FDIC), and the OCC into a single agency with a unified federal charter, merging the Securities and Exchange Commission (SEC) and the Commodity Futures Trading Commission (CFTC) into a single agency to oversee capital markets, and creating a federal insurance regulator. The proposed structure could clarify regulatory responsibility and reduce complexity and inefficiency.[33] More recently, the 2018 Treasury report on fintech and innovation included recommendations on agile regulation, regulatory sandboxes, and improving the clarity and efficiency of regulatory frameworks.[34]

In general, reducing fragmentation, overlapping jurisdiction, and duplicative regulatory functions would make U.S. financial regulation both more effective and more efficient. Fintech provides an opportunity, and in fact, an imperative, to streamline the system. The decisions on how to revise and improve regulation should be based on clear factual evidence, not as a reaction to industry pressure or ideological views. And regulatory review and improvement should be a continuous practice, just as it is in the United Kingdom.

Develop Broad Principles Instead of Restrictive Rules

No matter how well developed a policy or law is, the world does not stand still. Good policymakers have the judgment to consistently adapt to changing circumstances by updating their approach and regulations. This is especially important when technology is changing as quickly as it is today.

One good way to ensure adaptability is, when possible, to rely on broad principles of conduct, rather than restrictive rules, for regulation. One such principle would be to supervise like activity in like ways. This would mean that an entity making a small business loan would fall under the same guidelines for disclosure or conduct of its business, whether it is a bank or a nonbank lender. Basic tenets like those embodied in the Small Business Borrowers' Bill of Rights could be important foundational principles for more specific legislative or regulatory actions. One overarching principle might be to promote clear product disclosure in ways that customers find easy to understand and compare. A principles-based approach would also provide more consistency—and avoid conflicting or confusing guidance as different agencies make their own rules around data ownership and privacy.

Ensure Constructive Communication and Coordination Among Regulators

At a minimum, regulators should share relevant information with each other and coordinate their efforts whenever possible. Following the 2008 crisis, Congress recognized that fragmentation and lack of coordination were problems. They responded by creating the Financial Stability Oversight Council

(FSOC) in the Dodd-Frank Act as a forum for its member agencies to regularly meet to discuss issues of mutual concern. Another interagency body, the Federal Financial Institutions Examination Council (FFIEC), was established in 1979 with the goal of prescribing "uniform principles, standards and report forms for the federal examination of financial institutions." FSOC and FFIEC have been helpful, but coordination should be enhanced in other ways.

A 2014 Bipartisan Policy Center report recommended creating a consolidated task force made up of examiners from the OCC, the Fed, and the FDIC, who would jointly conduct their bank examinations. The relevant state bank regulatory agency would also have the option of joining the task force. The task force would submit a single set of questions to the entity being examined and publish a joint examination report that would be immediately available to each of the agencies involved.[35] Ideas such as this one would be excellent candidates for a pilot program—perhaps coordinated by FFIEC—to test them in practice.

There could also be better coordination on third-party vendors, as we have discussed in Chapter 10. If the agencies coordinated their guidance as much as possible and provided financial firms with single agency points of contact to streamline communication about third-party arrangements, they could ensure that the compliance burden is no greater than it needs to be. FFIEC could, for example, conduct regular trainings of examiners that are coordinated across all the regulatory agencies, so that examiners have the same criteria by which they administer third-party rules.

Use Innovation to Improve Regulation

Innovation is also important in regulatory compliance, where the use of regulatory technology, or "regtech," is growing. Regtech applications help in two ways. First, firms can increasingly use technology to ensure that they are complying with rules and other requirements. And regulators can use innovation to find more effective and less costly ways to audit compliance, find anomalies, and identify potential bad actors for further review. Some countries have even used regulatory sandboxes, and "sprints" and "hackathons," to solve specific compliance problems. In general, more data, more transparency, and more streamlining of activities are good watchwords in order for both regulators and policymakers to make continuous improvement in regulatory processes and outcomes.

*   *   *

Getting regulation right is difficult, as it requires balancing appropriate oversight with promoting innovation. Too little oversight could lead to the emergence of bad actors or another financial crisis that would hurt small businesses, while too much regulation could stifle new products and innovations that would make life easier for small businesses.

Unfortunately, while other countries have proactively sought out solutions to this dilemma, the United States must make up ground. But it is not too late for regulators to step up to the task. Indeed, how regulators respond to the challenges before them will determine whether the United States takes advantage of the enormous opportunity to lead in financial technology and innovation—and to help the nation's small businesses.

Conclusion

12

The Future of Fintech and the American Dream

Small businesses have been around since the time of early civilizations, and lending to small businesses is almost that old. The roots of traditional lending can be traced back to 3,000-year-old written loan contracts from Mesopotamia, which show the development of a credit system and include the concept of interest.

These ancient records include a loan to one Dumuzi-gamil, a bread distributor in the Mesopotamian city of Ur. He and his partner borrowed 500 grams of silver from the businessman Shumi-abum, who appeared to be acting as a banker. Dumuzi-gamil became a prominent bread distributor within the region by operating institutional bakeries that supplied the temple. In fact, one tablet describes him as the "grain supplier to the King." This early businessman paid an annual rate of 3.78 percent. Some of his colleagues were not as lucky. Other loans of silver to fisherman and farmers were documented at rates as high as 20 percent interest for a single month.[1]

Even 3,000 years ago, the structure of commercial activities required capital that the merchant could use to fund the business, and the owner of the capital required a return for the use of those resources. Remarkably, this initial contractual relationship still forms the foundation for the arrangements between small businesses and their lenders.

Small business lending has been so consistent over time because the basic math of small business operations has remained constant. A business sells a good or service for some margin over the cost of providing the product. Even in a high-margin business, the profits from each transaction are a small percentage of the sale. This makes it hard to accumulate the large amounts of capital that investments in land, animals, or supplies can require.

© The Author(s) 2018
K. G. Mills, *Fintech, Small Business & the American Dream*,
https://doi.org/10.1007/978-3-030-03620-1_12

Enter the small business lender, and the resulting arrangements of loan contracts, interest, and repayment over time. Over the centuries, many facets of these arrangements have evolved, with the establishment of money, banks, and traditional loan products such as term loans and lines of credit. But at their core, the needs of small businesses for capital have not changed.

Until recently, the modern market for small business capital had been operating adequately, though not optimally. Large and small banks in the United States provided various loan products and relationship activities designed to address the needs of small businesses for working capital and expansion investments. For most of the twentieth century, small business lending saw little innovation and only incrementally used technology to automate existing processes. The customer experience was slow and paper-intensive, but the market felt little pressure to change.

Not anymore. As we have seen, the financial crisis of 2008 and the entrance of new fintech competitors was a one-two punch that galvanized a new cycle of innovation in small business lending. The frozen credit markets showed the importance of small business lending to the economy and the slow recovery highlighted the market gaps. Entrepreneurs demonstrated that technology could change the built-in frictions in the traditional small business lending process, and a new era of innovation was born.

In this new era, we ask a final set of questions: what will the small business lending environment of the future look like? How will technology enable new products and activities to emerge? Will credit be more widely available? Will more small businesses be better off, or will many be taken advantage of by bad actors? Given the fundamentals of small business needs and the changes in the lending markets we have explored, what exactly will be different in the future—and what will stay the same?

Truths of Small Business Lending

Change is flourishing in small business lending because the innovators are finding new ways to address some of the fundamental barriers or frictions in the marketplace. These frictions have been there for a long time and have been hard to ameliorate. They have been so constant that we call them the "truths" of small business lending.

The first truth is that not all businesses succeed. In fact, small businesses fail at an alarming rate. Over 50 percent of businesses started in the United States over the last 10 years failed before they reached the fifth year. Providing a loan to most of these businesses would not have been a good idea because they failed for some reason other than lack of credit. Often, their product or idea was something that customers did not want, or something that they could not deliver profitably.

Even in the most robust economic times, when credit is relatively easy to obtain, an estimated 50 percent of loan applications are denied because the small business is not creditworthy. If such a business were to get a loan and fail, that loan would turn into an additional burden the owner would be desperately trying to pay off. Thus, the goal is not to get loans to every small business, but to those who are creditworthy, meaning that they will be able to effectively use the capital to help themselves succeed. A related objective is to pair each creditworthy owner with a loan that fits their business: one that is the right amount, duration, and cost, with terms that the borrower can successfully handle and repay.

The second truth is that it is difficult to know who is creditworthy. Many small business owners do not understand their cash flows well and, as a result, can suffer unexpected cash shortages. Businesses sometimes need cash to bridge a slow period, and sometimes they need funds because they are doing better than expected. One of the least understood realities of growth in a business is that it usually requires cash to fund increases in working capital or fixed assets. Thus, a fast-growing business can run out of cash, and even fail, if it does not plan ahead for a way to access the credit it will need.

Lenders have a hard time determining whether a small business owner is creditworthy for two reasons that we have discussed earlier. The first is their information opacity. It is hard to know if a small business is profitable, especially given that they often don't know themselves. The second issue is their heterogeneity, the fact that all small businesses are different. Because of this heterogeneity, it is hard to generate that "truth file"—the formula that can automatically give a credit approval to a loan applicant. In traditional small business lending, a banker might spend weeks with a small business, understanding their operations, only to ask at the end for a personal guarantee. A corollary to the second truth is that bankers seek collateral whenever possible, especially when the prospects of a business are opaque.

These two truths are the foundations for the story we have told in this book. Despite the importance of small business to the economy, lending to small businesses hasn't changed much because this lending is risky, and the information issues make the loan process costly and difficult to automate. Bankers have compensated by viewing the business as an extension of the business owner, and making personal guarantees the standard for anyone but the most creditworthy.

These longstanding frictions in the small business lending market have been the most difficult for newer or smaller businesses, because these businesses are the hardest to understand, have the least collateral, and are the most likely to fail. But most of the 30 million U.S. small businesses are indeed small and, if they seek capital, are likely to want small loans. The result is gaps and inefficiencies in the marketplace, and creditworthy borrowers who are either rejected or discouraged from getting the capital they need.

The Future of Small Business Lending

The technology that is available today has the power to create information and intelligence to which small business owners and their lenders have never before had access. This should improve the small business lending market in fundamental ways.

What Will Change in the Future?

Let's imagine a future state in which lenders and borrowers have much better and more transparent information, and there is an active and fluid market matching supply and demand for loans. What would be the benefits of a more perfect market for small business lending, and what risks and uncertainties could undermine its functioning?

Better Matching

In this market, big data and artificial intelligence would play a central role, helping lenders determine whether a small business borrower is going to succeed. If technology can significantly improve the ability to differentiate creditworthy from noncreditworthy borrowers, everyone will benefit. Lenders who have greater clarity on which borrowers are poor credit risks would avoid piling more debt onto those who will be unable to pay it back, which in turn would allow them to lend to creditworthy borrowers at lower cost.

Reduced Gaps

In a market with perfect information, there would be no gap in access to credit for any borrower who met the credit criteria. The result: more creditworthy businesses would be funded, particularly those seeking small-dollar loans. Square's average loan size of $6,000 has meant that many retailers who never before had access to capital can buy the piece of equipment they need to operate. The lower costs of automated transactions would allow even these small loans to be made profitably.

Of course, in reality, perfect or complete information is unlikely to exist. No data source will capture the entrepreneurial talent of the small business owner, which may be a critical factor in the business's success. It may be impossible to fully replicate the input of a relationship banker who knows the borrower personally. But the marketplace is now crowded with fintech innovators, large technology companies, and traditional banks who are turning over new ground in finding data that has predictive ability. Recall the story of Tala from Chapter 8. Operating in the developing world, the company uses data gleaned from Android phones to predict the creditworthiness of shop owners who have no formal credit history or banking relationship. They successfully make loans as low as $100, opening the door to more economic opportunity for those business owners.

In the United States, no one knows the size of the gap in access to credit or what the improvement would look like if technology made markets work optimally. But even with small improvements, tens of thousands of small businesses could be affected.[2] At the margin, technology is likely to help lenders find more creditworthy borrowers, and the reduction in frictions in the user experience should make borrowers' search costs lower, and make it easier for them to find a loan.

Lower Search Costs

The perfect small business lending market will offer a better customer experience. We have already seen applications that are short and easy to fill out, supported by automated data access through application programming interfaces (APIs). Small businesses that used to spend 25 hours on an application now have a fully digital experience and a near immediate response. For small businesses who have been deterred by the time commitment and length of the process, new lending marketplaces of the future will be more open, transparent, and usable. This should bring more borrowers into the process and improve their ability to get matched with a loan if they meet the lending criteria.

Transparency and Choice

Comparison shopping with full transparency and choice will be part of the future small business loan market. Borrowers will be able to understand the costs, benefits, and risks of loan options, and be able to compare those options on an apples-to-apples basis. We are already seeing this story play out in the personal credit card space. In the 1990s, almost all credit card offers came to consumers in the mail or could be found at bank branches. Then, in the early 2000s, banks began offering products online, which allowed consumers to shop and compare from the comfort of their own homes. Now, shopping sites like CreditCards.com, Credit Karma, and NerdWallet are providing aggregation services that enable consumers to compare prices and shop bank by bank online. Consumers have complete information written in plain English about all available products, pricing, and approval odds in a central location. Although small business loan products are more complicated, comparison marketplaces such as Fundera and Lendio already exist, and their functionality will improve. The question facing credit providers in this new environment will be, as one investor puts it, "Would a rational consumer armed with perfect information choose your product?"[3]

Risk-Based Pricing

In a perfectly functioning market, every small business who wanted a loan could get one—if three conditions were true:

1. Business owners were sophisticated and well-informed enough to understand the full costs of the loan, both the monetary costs and the "life" costs. That would mean borrowers were able to rationally assess the consequences of failure, as well as success for themselves and their families.
2. Lenders were incentivized both economically and by regulation to create full disclosure about all loan fees and costs.[4]
3. Lenders were able to perfectly match the price of credit with the risk of the credit offered.

If these three principles were operating, then theoretically, the market would match the risk of each loan with a price. If the borrower was willing to pay that price, the loan would be made. It would be the personal choice and responsibility of each small business owner to decide if the cost was too high.

This marketplace may be where we are heading. Certain fintech innovators are offering higher-priced loans than banks are comfortable making. Some borrowers, such as Linda Pagan of The Hat Shop NYC in Chapter 5, are happy to take those loans, as they meet their needs.

But risk-based pricing and a free market solution for small business lending comes with several concerns. Behavioral economists have demonstrated that humans are wired to downplay long-term negative consequences and overemphasize short-term wins. Entrepreneurs and small business owners are even more likely than most to have an optimistic view of the potential future outcomes. If small business owners were not generally optimistic, far fewer would take the risk of starting a business in the first place. Will these entrepreneurs be able to rationally assess the future risks of loan defaults, or will they just take the money and believe it will all work out well?

The high costs of some loans in the fintech market raise another question: what level of pricing are we willing to tolerate in the market? Should there be caps, or should we allow the levels to be set by the market and let borrowers use their own judgment in taking on loans? Although there are sharp disagreements on these questions, logic says that at some point, the costs will simply be too much for the small business owner to ever repay.

The risk of debt traps has long been recognized by usury laws and more recent efforts to regulate payday lenders. Yet, some argue that a fast short-term cash option can be a necessary lifeline for a business, even if it is costly. Leaning on the side of a cap on rates, and living with the market inefficiencies, is perhaps a better solution than allowing too many small businesses to fall prey to overly optimistic forecasts, and end up losing their businesses and maybe more. An interest rate cap or limit is particularly appropriate in an environment without full transparency of loan terms and small business borrower protections.

The Perfect Information Platform

The Small Business Utopia described in Chapter 8 includes an information platform for small businesses that gives them better insights into the financial side of their businesses. In particular, we imagined this dashboard integrating information flows from bank statements, payment activities, past sales, and expense patterns to predict cash flows and potential shortfalls. With a more fluid lending market in operation, different credit options would also be available at the push of a button, and an automated "bot" would dispense financial advice. In the ideal world, this system would be augmented by human advisors who would build a relationship with the small business owner and provide timely counsel and insight on a more personal basis.

Anyone who has run a small business or interacted with small business owners knows that, despite their abilities and talents, it is hard to carry an integrated financial picture of the business in one's head. QuickBooks, Xero, and other accounting software have helped, but many entrepreneurs operate by instinct, supplemented by scraps of paper. The frictions and inefficiencies of this less than perfect manual process would be transformed by a solution that includes the three elements described above: a dashboard that integrates financial information streams, simple access to loan products, and personal and automated advice. With these tools, it is likely that fewer businesses would fail, at least from unexpected cash surprises or mismanagement of their cash positions.

The Voice of Small Business

Small businesses don't go unnoticed, but sometimes they do go unheard. As we noted at the beginning of Chapter 2, small businesses have a special place in the hearts of Americans, and are one of the few areas where there is bipartisan agreement. But the voice of small business is sometimes missing at the table. Small business owners are an independent, diverse group, and are busy running their companies, so they rarely convene and express their priorities. We saw this in the slowness of the banks' response to the pain points of their customers in the traditional lending experience.

There are signs, however, that more attention is being paid to the voices of small businesses. In 2009, Jack Dorsey founded Square, based largely on a desire to make life work better for small businesses. Each day in San Francisco, he would walk to work by a different route so he could observe small business owners opening their doors and going about their daily tasks.[5] His focus translated into Square, a device that allowed them to easily process credit card payments, and then Square Capital. Other new entrants like the payroll and benefits operator Gusto, and the accounting software provider Xero, see small businesses as important customers, and innovate every day to more effectively meet their needs.

Technology is also enabling small businesses to be a more connected community. A new Boston-based company, Alignable, has built a series of online networks for small business owners. In over 30,000 locations, the Alignable platform lets 3 million small businesses advise each other, sharing issues they face and solutions they find helpful.[6] Often, they refer businesses to each other, or just brainstorm answers to questions posed on the community forum. Perhaps this kind of vibrant small business online community is one of the new alternative sources of relationship advice. It will certainly have an impact on the spread of good ideas, products, or companies that provide solutions for small business problems.

The Dark Side of the Black Box

The use of big data and algorithms will bring new products and services, but also bring some new concerns. It is not yet clear what impact the changes we anticipate from technology will have on access to capital for traditionally underserved markets. In the past, women and minorities have struggled to find willing lenders. The hope is that with more efficient markets and new data sources, more creditworthy borrowers from underserved segments of the market will get loans. However, "black box" algorithms, where the formulas are not open to review, could lead to an outcome of more discrimination, not less.

One way to get ahead of these concerns is to collect the actual data on access to capital in the small business market. The most relevant metrics would be loan origination data by size of loan and by type of small business owner. As we have discussed, the law requiring this data collection was passed after the financial crisis, but has yet to be implemented.[7] More innovation can take place if there is a way to track potential poor market outcomes. Collecting this information and using it to identify and correct market gaps is a critical foundational element of a highly functioning small business credit market, as artificial intelligence becomes an integral part of lending decisions.

The Role of Government

With the insights from better information in hand, government can play a more effective role in intervening when there are market gaps. Programs such as Community Development Financial Institutions (CDFIs), the Small Business Administration (SBA), and many state and local initiatives already play this role, often with great impact. In the future, banks could use Community Reinvestment Act (CRA) funds more effectively to target market failures in small business lending and improve access.

The government must also ensure that small businesses are not taken advantage of by bad actors amidst the new opportunities. The early days of fintech saw the emergence of high cost products with hidden fees and brokers with misaligned incentives. As we have argued earlier, Washington needs to take steps through a more effective regulatory environment to protect small business owners with the same vigor as they do consumers.

Predictions for the Future of Fintech and Small Business Lending

What is going to happen next? Of course, we don't know for sure. But based on the narrative described in the preceding chapters, it is possible to make some predictions:

Prediction #1: Data Ownership Will Determine the Level of Innovation in Small Business Platforms

We have described a new state of Small Business Utopia, where information streams come together to provide a more transparent, helpful, and predictive view of a small business's cash and financial needs. This data integration will improve how small businesses decide what capital they need, how lenders assess whether they want to lend, and how efficiently the marketplace matches the parties. At the margin, this enhanced information will increase the success rates of small business owners, who will be able to plan for and manage unexpected cash fluctuations.

Who will provide the integrated platform?

The answer will depend on an unlikely source—regulation of data ownership. If banks, or even large tech companies, control customer financial data, then they will likely be the central facilitators of an integrated data platform. Some view this as a big mistake. Brad Kitschke, the CEO of FinTech Australia, said, "Allowing the big banks to control or restrict access is not in the interests of consumers. Without access to this data, consumers will continue to be forced to accept the off-the-shelf generic products on offer from the big banks that don't meet their needs."[8]

In Europe and the United Kingdom, recent legislation has given control of data to the customer. We believe this structure will drive more innovation. As the fintech, Plaid, has demonstrated, new infrastructure can be created behind the scenes to integrate data streams into useful formats. This will allow innovators to access relevant data with customers' permission, and create platforms that fundamentally change the way small businesses operate financially. Banks and other financial firms could then use these solutions, or create their own, but would not control the data at the source. We should carefully watch the countries who have already adopted Open Banking, as their experiences will undoubtedly provide useful lessons on what decisions to make and what mistakes to avoid.

It is not at all certain that the United States will ever implement Open Banking regulation. Banks and large tech companies have vested interests in controlling data, and there is no momentum for new data privacy legislation in the current environment. This may change if powerful innovation occurs, such as the dashboards and other tools we have described, or if other pressures build on the side of data security. As we navigate these waters, it is worth remembering that the theories of markets and competition support the prediction that more control of data in the hands of customers rather than large institutions is likely to lead to more experimentation and opportunity for products and services that transform small businesses' lives.

Prediction #2: There Will Be Small Business Banks

The narrative of this book begins with the fact that small businesses are important, but often get less attention than they deserve. In lending, small business products and services are sometimes treated as the poor cousins of larger consumer lending divisions. In the future, this will not be the case. The future winners in small business lending will be the players, new or old, that focus on understanding and serving the unique needs and operations of small businesses. With low-cost digital banks able to serve a national footprint, specialized banks providing best in class services will become a new competitive factor.

These small business banks of the future will provide an integrated gateway to loans, lines of credit, payments platforms, business intelligence, and numerous other products and services. They will create easy to use digital experiences that cater to the time-strapped small business owner and automate functions that used to require paperwork or a physical trip to the branch. Yet, they will not abandon personal relationships. Whether it is by telephone, online, or in person, the successful players will find ways to feed the insatiable need of small business owners for personal advice and counsel. The solutions could be as traditional as the Chase BizMobile™ bus (Chapter 8) or as new as the peer advisory groups on Alignable's small business network.

As online banks take hold, there will be small business banks with vertical specializations. By focusing on specific industries, these banks will improve their expertise in underwriting and their ability to deliver more customized services and advice. For example, imagine new financial services entities ready to support restaurants, electricians, or dentists, and building custom financial dashboards and loan products adapted to that small business segment. As the best solutions emerge, word of mouth, facilitated by online small business communities, will send customers flocking to the provider.

In the longer term, digitization in small business credit will put pressure on borrowing rates and profit margins. As options are increasingly transparent and comparable, business owners will be able to more easily find their way to products that meet their needs. As demonstrated by some consumer sectors such as insurance and mortgages, this trend will commoditize products and services as customers demand comparable features and simple interactions. Banks and other financial services providers will need to have at least a base level of competitive loan products and be conduits to other specialized options if they want to maintain their role as the primary source of capital to small businesses in the future.

Prediction #3: Regulation Will Fail to Keep Up

While it would be ideal for policymakers to be proactive, history shows that human nature is more often prone to reaction. Congress in particular is a reactive body, if only because voters reward elected officials for responding to problems, rather than preventing them from happening. U.S. financial regulatory agencies have the advantage of greater independence from Congress and the executive branch, including independent funding in some cases. This gives them greater latitude to be proactive, and sometimes they are. But fixing the fragmented structure of U.S. financial regulation, with its overlapping and duplicative jurisdictions, will require well-coordinated, forward-thinking policy and true bipartisan commitment.

Therefore, we expect that regulation will struggle to keep up, to the detriment of the market, allowing bad actors to prey on unsuspecting small businesses and fueling a confusing and costly regulatory environment. Unintended consequences in a world of increased data usage, such as privacy issues and disparate impact, will also result if policymaking does not become more proactive.

Fintech, Small Business & the American Dream

The view of this book is largely optimistic. Additional data and efforts to innovate in small business lending markets are generally good trends, which we predict will have a positive impact on small business outcomes. The entry of fintech entrepreneurs has awakened the competitive instincts of banks and traditional lenders, who have realized that they don't want to cede the small business market to the new disruptors. Large technology companies have also demonstrated that they view small business lending as an important place to play. This heightened competition is good for small businesses, who too often have been an afterthought for lenders, in the shadow of consumers and large businesses.

Of course, the full picture of the future is not entirely rosy. The U.S. regulatory system in its present state is ill-equipped to protect small business owners, and political realities seem likely to prevent simplification of the current morass of rules. Nonetheless, we could be on the brink of one of the most positive transformations in small business lending in at least a century. As new entrepreneurs enter, and older players innovate, the attention will be on understanding what small businesses want and delivering new options that will make it easier for small businesses to succeed.

There is a long debate within economics about the degree to which finance causes economic growth, as opposed to just following economic activity. In a seminal 1997 article, Ross Levine outlined several key functions performed by the financial sector that drive economic growth, including allocating capital.[9] Levine saw the development of financial markets as a critical influence on growth, and not as an inconsequential or passive "side show." Thus, innovations that reduce frictions in critical functions like lending and make financial markets work better are a positive force that should drive more prosperity. From the evidence we see today, fintech may be just such a force for small business lending and the small businesses that depend on America's financial markets for their growth and success.

∗   ∗   ∗

Ten years ago, Ron Siegel decided to start a bakery, and wondered what he would call his new business. "It was difficult and scary to break out of my daily work routine to pursue a dream that had an unknown outcome," Ron said. "The name 'When Pigs Fly' means 'I doubt it's possible' and that's why it was the perfect name for my bakery."[10] Today, Ron tells his story on the packages of millions of loaves of his bread. And following in the footsteps of Dumuzi-gamil, our bread distributor from Mesopotamia, "When Pigs Fly" sells its bread all over New England from its operating plant in York, Maine.

The American spirit of entrepreneurship has been a defining element since the founding of our nation. Today, innovators have brought new ideas and technology to the small business lending market and, as we have described in this book, a consequential transformation has begun. The outlook for small businesses is getting brighter, as these changes create more opportunities for people like Ron to do what often seems impossible—open and operate a small business and successfully pursue the American Dream.

Notes

Chapter 1

1. Interview with Frank Rotman of QED Investors, April 13, 2018.
2. The Dodd-Frank Wall Street Reform and Consumer Protection Act was the U.S. Congress' main legislative action that changed regulations after the financial crisis of 2008.

Chapter 2

1. Lydia Saad, "Military, Small Business, Police Still Stir Most Confidence," *Gallup*, June 28, 2018, https://news.gallup.com/poll/236243/military-small-business-police-stir-confidence.aspx.
2. https://www.youtube.com/watch?v=00wQYmvfhn4.
3. Paul M. Romer, "Implementing a National Technology Strategy with Self-Organizing Industry Investment Boards," *Brookings Papers on Economic Activity: Microeconomics*, no. 2 (1993): 345, https://www.brookings.edu/wp-content/uploads/1993/01/1993b_bpeamicro_romer.pdf.
4. Robert Atkinson and Howard Wial, "Boosting Productivity, Innovation, and Growth through a National Innovation Foundation," *Brookings Institution and Information Technology and Innovation Foundation*, April 2008, https://www.brookings.edu/wp-content/uploads/2016/06/NIF-Report.pdf.

© The Author(s) 2018
K. G. Mills, *Fintech, Small Business & the American Dream*,
https://doi.org/10.1007/978-3-030-03620-1

5. J.A. Schumpeter, *The Theory of Economic Development* (Cambridge, MA: Cambridge University Press, 1934).

6. Erik Hurst and Benjamin Wild Pugsley, "What Do Small Businesses Do?," *Brookings Papers on Economic Activity, 2011*, no. 2 (2011), https://www.brookings.edu/wp-content/uploads/2011/09/2011b_bpea_hurst.pdf.

7. J. John Wu and Robert D. Atkinson, "How Technology-Based Startups Support U.S. Economic Growth," *Information Technology and Innovation Foundation*, November 2017, https://itif.org/publications/2017/11/28/how-technology-based-start-ups-support-us-economic-growth.

8. "Consumers Now More Willing to Go Out of Their Way to Support Small Businesses," *UPS Store*, May 12, 2014, https://www.theupsstore.com/about/pressroom/consumers-support-small-businesses.

9. "American Express Teams Up with Shaquille O'Neal and Friends to Drive Card Members to Shop Small and Earn Big Rewards," *American Express*, November 10, 2016, https://about.americanexpress.com/press-release/american-express-teams-shaquille-oneal-and-friends-drive-card-members-shop-small-and.

10. "MIT Work of the Future: Perspectives from Business and Economics," Video (Cambridge, MA: MIT Technology Review, 2018), https://www.technologyreview.com/video/611340/mit-work-of-the-future-perspectives-from-business-and-economics/. Note: Solow observes that the share of national income going to wages and salaries has fallen from 75 percent to 62 percent over the past few decades, perhaps requiring that we change our paradigm when it comes to jobs being the main way the economy drives income distribution.

11. "United States Small Business Profile, 2018," *U.S. Small Business Administration Office of Advocacy*, 2018, https://www.sba.gov/sites/default/files/advocacy/2018-Small-Business-Profiles-US.pdf.

12. "Frequently Asked Questions about Small Business," *U.S. Small Business Administration Office of Advocacy*, August 2018, https://www.sba.gov/sites/default/files/advocacy/Frequently-Asked-Questions-Small-Business-2018.pdf.

13. "Business Employment Dynamics—Table E. Quarterly Net Change by Firm Size Class, Seasonally Adjusted," *Bureau of Labor Statistics*, last modified July 25, 2018, https://www.bls.gov/bdm/bdmfirmsize.htm.

14. David Madland, "Growth and the Middle Class," *Democracy Journal*, no. 20 (Spring 2011), https://democracyjournal.org/magazine/20/growth-and-the-middle-class/.

15. William Easterly, "The Middle Class Consensus and Economic Development," *Journal of Economic Growth* 6, no. 4 (July 2001): 317–335, https://williameasterly.files.wordpress.com/2010/08/34_easterly_middleclassconsensus_prp.pdf.

16. Ben Hubbard and Kate Kelly, "Saudi Arabia's Grand Plan to Move Beyond Oil: Big Goals, Bigger Hurdles," *New York Times*, October 25, 2017, https://www.nytimes.com/2017/10/25/world/middleeast/saudi-arabias-grand-plan-to-move-beyond-oil-big-goals-bigger-hurdles.html.

17. Daron Acemoglu, Ufuk Akcigit, Harun Alp, Nicholas Bloom, and William Kerr, "Innovation, Reallocation and Growth," *Becker Friedman Institute for Research in Economics Working Paper*, no. 21, December 1, 2017, https://papers.ssrn.com/sol3/papers.cfm?abstract_id=3079898.

18. Edward L. Glaeser, Sari Pekkala Kerr, and William R. Kerr, "Entrepreneurship and Urban Growth: An Empirical Assessment with Historical Mines," *Review of Economics and Statistics* 97, no. 2, May 2015, https://www.mitpressjournals.org/doi/abs/10.1162/REST_a_00456?journalCode=rest.

19. Anthony Breitzman and Diana Hicks, "An Analysis of Small Business Patents by Industry and Firm Size," *SBA Advocacy*, no. 335 (2008): 6, https://rdw.rowan.edu/cgi/viewcontent.cgi?referer=https://www.google.com/&httpsredir=1&article=1011&context=csm_facpub.

20. Mirjam Van Praag and Peter H. Versloot, "What is the Value of Entrepreneurship? A Review of Recent Research," *Small Business Economics*, no. 29 (2007): 351–382, https://link.springer.com/content/pdf/10.1007%2Fs11187-007-9074-x.pdf.

21. William R. Kerr, Ramana Nanda, and Matthew Rhodes-Kropf, "Entrepreneurship as Experimentation," *Journal of Economic Perspectives* 28, no. 3 (Summer 2014): 25–48, https://pubs.aeaweb.org/doi/pdfplus/10.1257/jep.28.3.25.

22. Elizabeth Brown and Austin Nichols, "Self-Employment, Family-Business Ownership, and Economic Mobility," *Urban Institute*, May 2014, https://www.urban.org/sites/default/files/publication/33841/413134-self-employment-family-business-ownership-and-economic-mobility.pdf.

23. Ben R. Craig, William E. Jackson, and James B. Thomson, "Small Firm Finance, Credit Rationing, and the Impact of SBA-Guaranteed Lending on Local Economic Growth," *Journal of Small Business Management* 45, no. 1 (2007): 116–132, https://papers.ssrn.com/sol3/papers.cfm?abstract_id=984724.

24. William R. Kerr, *The Gift of Global Talent: How Migration Shapes Business, Economy & Society* (Palo Alto, CA: Stanford University Press, 2018).

25. "The 2017 Kauffman Index of Startup Activity: National Trends," *Kauffman Foundation*, May 2017, https://www.kauffman.org/kauffman-index/reporting/startup-activity.

26. Adam Bluestein, "The Most Entrepreneurial Group in America Wasn't Born in America," *Inc.*, February 2015, https://www.inc.com/magazine/201502/adam-bluestein/the-most-entrepreneurial-group-in-america-wasnt-born-in-america.html.

27. "United States Small Business Profile, 2018," *U.S. Small Business Administration Office of Advocacy*, 2018, https://www.sba.gov/sites/default/files/advocacy/2018-Small-Business-Profiles-US.pdf.

28. Note: In 2016, 15.4 million people were reported as self-employed. Some of them operated firms that had employees. However, given that there were only 5.9 million employer firms in 2016, most of the self-employed were likely also non-employer firms. As an estimate, 12 million or approximately half of the 24 million non-employer firms were full-time jobs for their owners, while the others were side businesses. Data for "Nonemployer businesses" is taken from the Nonemployer Statistics at the U.S. Census Bureau (https://www.census.gov/programs-surveys/nonemployer-statistics/data/tables.All.html); Data for Unincorporated Nonemployer Businesses is taken from the Bureau of Labor Statistics table on Self-employed workers, unincorporated (not seasonally adjusted), (https://www.bls.gov/webapps/legacy/cpsatab9.htm).

29. Note: Aggregate firm data is taken from the Census Bureau's Statistics of U.S. Businesses (SUSB) data tables: https://www.census.gov/programs-surveys/susb.html. Subcategories are derived from the supply chain categorization of the economy developed in Mercedes Delgado and Karen G. Mills, "A New Categorization of the U.S. Economy: The Role of Supply Chain Industries in Innovation and Economic Performance," MIT Sloan Research Paper, no. 5241-16, December 11, 2018, http://dx.doi.org/10.2139/ssrn.3050296. The supplier category includes only supply chain traded firms. For the purpose of this figure, supply chain local firms are included in the Main Street category.

30. Lawrence F. Katz and Alan B. Krueger, "The Rise and Nature of Alternative Work Arrangements in the United States, 1995–2015," *National Bureau of Economic Research*, September 2016, http://www.nber.org/papers/w22667.

31. Ian Hathaway and Mark Muro, "Tracking the Gig Economy: New Numbers," *Brookings*, October 2016, https://www.brookings.edu/research/tracking-the-gig-economy-new-numbers/.

32. Note: For example, from 2016 to 2017, the number of non-employer businesses grew by 482,000, while the number of self-employed grew by 179,000.

33. Mercedes Delgado and Karen Mills, "A New Categorization of the U.S. Economy: The Role of Supply Chain Industries in Innovation and Economic Performance," *MIT Sloan Research Paper*, no. 5241–16, December 11, 2018, http://dx.doi.org/10.2139/ssrn.3050296. Note: This paper estimates a new industry categorization that separates supply chain (SC) industries (i.e. those that sell primarily to businesses or government) from business-to-consumer (B2C) industries (i.e. those that sell primarily to consumers). To our knowledge, this is the first systematic quantification of the supply chain economy. The supply chain includes both manufacturers, and importantly, service providers. It is a large and distinct sector with higher wages and a higher degree of innovative capacity than B2C industries. See also: Mercedes Delgado and Karen Mills, "Policy Briefing: The Supply Chain Economy: A New Framework for Understanding Innovation and Services," October 2017, https://innovation.mit.edu/assets/MITii_Lab_Supply-Chain-Economy_FINAL.pdf.
34. Mercedes Delgado and Michael E. Porter, "Clusters and the Great Recession," June 8, 2017, http://mitsloan.mit.edu/shared/ods/documents/Fang_L_CV_web_09-19-2014.pdf?DocumentID=4075.
35. Aaron Chatterji, Edward L. Glaeser, and William R. Kerr, "Clusters of Entrepreneurship and Innovation," *NBER Working Paper*, no. 19013, May 2013, https://www.nber.org/papers/w19013.
36. John Reid Blackwell, "Rolls-Royce Could Employ Up to 500 in Prince George," *Richmond Times-Dispatch*, October 20, 2009, https://www.richmond.com/business/rolls-royce-could-employ-up-to-in-prince-george/article_a238c9f9-bc24-5c67-a42e-0d643ab5df03.html.
37. Jorge Guzman and Scott Stern, "Nowcasting and Placecasting Entrepreneurial Quality and Performance," *NBER Working Paper*, no. 20952, February 2015, http://www.nber.org/papers/w20954.
38. Ramana Nanda, "Financing High-Potential Entrepreneurship," *IZA World of Labor*, 2016, https://wol.iza.org/articles/financing-high-potential-entrepreneurship.
39. Ryan Decker, John Haltiwanger, Ron S. Jarmin, and Javier Miranda, "The Secular Decline in Business Dynamism in the U.S," *University of Maryland Working Paper*, June 2014, http://econweb.umd.edu/~haltiwan/DHJM_6_2_2014.pdf.
40. John Haltiwanger, Ron S. Jarmin, and Javier Miranda, "Who Creates Jobs? Small Versus Large Versus Young," *The Review of Economics and Statistics* 95, no. 2 (2013), https://www.mitpressjournals.org/doi/10.1162/REST_a_00288.
41. Jason Wiens and Chris Jackson, "The Importance of Young Firms for Economic Growth," *Ewing Marion Kauffman Foundation Entrepreneurship*

Policy Digest, September 2015, http://www.kauffman.org/what-we-do/resources/entrepreneurship-policy-digest/the-importance-of-young-firms-for-economic-growth.

42. Ryan Decker, John Haltiwanger, Ron Jarmin, and Javier Miranda, "The Role of Entrepreneurship in US Job Creation and Economic Dynamism," *The Journal of Economic Perspectives* 28, no. 3 (2014): 3–24, https://pubs.aeaweb.org/doi/pdfplus/10.1257/jep.28.3.3.

43. Faith Karahan, Benjamin Pugsley, and Aysegül Sahin, "Understanding the 30-year Decline in the Startup Rate: A General Equilibrium Approach," May 2015, http://conference.iza.org/conference_files/EntreRes2015/pugsley_b22364.pdf.

44. Jan W. Rivkin, Karen G. Mills, and Michael E. Porter, "The Challenge of Shared Prosperity: Findings of Harvard Business School's 2015 Survey on American Competitiveness," Harvard Business School, September 2015, http://www.hbs.edu/competitiveness/Documents/challenge-of-shared-prosperity.pdf.

45. Karthik Krishnan and Pinshuo Wang, "The Cost of Financing Education: Can Student Debt Hinder Entrepreneurship?" *Forthcoming, Management Science*, November 2017, https://papers.ssrn.com/sol3/papers.cfm?abstract_id=2586378; Brent Ambrose, Larry Cordell, and Shuwei Ma, "The Impact of Student Loan Debt on Small Business Formation," *Federal Reserve Board of Philadelphia Working Paper*, no. 15–26, July 2015, https://papers.ssrn.com/sol3/papers.cfm?abstract_id=2633951.

Chapter 3

1. Interview with Pilar Guzman Zavala, August 31, 2017.

2. Nancy Dahlberg, "Passion, Perseverance Powered Empanada Maker through Tough Start," *Miami Herald*, July 10, 2016, http://www.miami-herald.com/news/business/biz-monday/article88785767.html.

3. Author's analysis of data from the Business Dynamics Statistics, *U.S. Census Bureau*, last modified September 23, 2015, https://www.census.gov/ces/dataproducts/bds/data_firm.html.

4. Mark Gertler and Simon Gilchrist, "Monetary Policy, Business Cycles, and the Behavior of Small Manufacturing Firms," *The Quarterly Journal of Economics* 109, no. 2 (May 1994), http://www.uh.edu/~bsorense/Gertler&Gilchrist.MP%20business%20cycles%20and%20behavior%20of%20small%20manufactoring%20firms.pdf; Randall S. Kroszner, Luc Laeven, and Daniela Klingebiel, "Banking Crises, Financial Dependence

and Growth," *Journal of Financial Economics* 84, no. 1 (2007), http://www.sciencedirect.com/science/article/pii/S0304405X0600208X; Gert Wehinger, "SMEs and the Credit Crunch: Current Financing Difficulties, Policy Measures, and a Review of Literature," *OECD Journal: Financial Market Trends*, no. 2 (2013), https://www.oecd.org/finance/SMEs-Credit-Crunch-Financing-Difficulties.pdf.

5. Diana Farrell and Chris Wheat, "Cash Is King: Flows, Balances, and Buffer Days: Evidence from 600,000 Small Businesses," JPMorgan Chase and Co. Institute, September 2016, https://www.jpmorganchase.com/content/dam/jpmorganchase/en/legacy/corporate/institute/document/jpmc-institute-small-business-report.pdf.

6. "2017 Small Business Credit Survey: Report on Employer Firms," *Federal Reserve Banks*, May 2018, p. 6, https://www.fedsmallbusiness.org/medialibrary/fedsmallbusiness/files/2018/sbcs-employer-firms-report.pdf.

7. Brian S. Chen, Samuel G. Hanson, and Jeremy C. Stein, "The Decline of Big-Bank Lending to Small Business: Dynamic Impacts on Local Credit and Labor Markets," *NBER Working Paper*, no. 23843, September 2017, http://www.nber.org/papers/w23843.

8. Roisin McCord, Edward Simpson Prescott, and Tim Sablik, "Explaining the Decline in the Number of Banks Since the Great Recession," EB15-03 (March 2015), https://www.richmondfed.org/~/media/richmondfedorg/publications/research/economic_brief/2015/pdf/eb_15-03.pdf.

9. "FDIC Community Banking Study," *Community Banking Initiative*, December 2012, https://www.fdic.gov/regulations/resources/cbi/study.html.

10. Mark Gertler and Simon Gilchrist, "Monetary Policy, Business Cycles, and the Behavior of Small Manufacturing Firms," *The Quarterly Journal of Economics* 109, no. 2 (May 1994), http://www.uh.edu/~bsorense/Gertler&Gilchrist.MP%20business%20cycles%20and%20behavior%20of%20small%20manufactoring%20firms.pdf.

11. Randall S. Kroszner, Luc Laeven, and Daniela Klingebiel, "Banking Crises, Financial Dependence and Growth," *Journal of Financial Economics* 84, no. 1 (2007), http://www.sciencedirect.com/science/article/pii/S0304405X0600208X.

12. Burcu Duygan-Bump, Alexey Levkov, and Judit Montoriol-Garriga, "Financing Constraints and Unemployment: Evidence from the Great Recession," *Federal Reserve Bank of Boston Working Paper*, no. QAU10-6 (December 2011), https://www.bostonfed.org/publications/risk-and-policy-analysis/2010/financing-constraints-and-unemployment-evidence-from-the-great-recession.aspx.

13. Gabriel Chodorow-Reich, "The Employment Effects of Credit Market Disruptions: Firm-level Evidence from the 2008–9 Financial Crisis," *Quarterly Journal of Economics* 129, no. 1 (2014): 1–59, https://scholar.harvard.edu/chodorow-reich/publications/employment-effects-credit-market-disruptions-firm-level-evidence-2008-09.

14. Note: The Federal Insurance Deposit Commission (FDIC) requires banks to file quarterly call reports which include total assets on bank balance sheets by loan size, but do not include loan origination data. Thus, they describe the stock of loans but not the flows.

15. Interview with George Osborne, September 2016.

16. Author's analysis of data from "Loans to Small Businesses and Small Farms," *Federal Deposit Insurance Corporation Quarterly Banking Profile*, accessed August 23, 2018, https://www.fdic.gov/bank/analytical/qbp/.

17. Note: The Small Business Administration Loan Guaranty Program allows banks to make small business loans with the promise that if the borrower defaults, the federal government will bear a designated portion of the loss.

18. Robert Jay Dilger, "Small Business Administration 7(a) Loan Guaranty Program," *Congressional Research Service*, November 7, 2018, https://fas.org/sgp/crs/misc/R41146.pdf.

19. Karen Gordon Mills and Brayden McCarthy, "The State of Small Business Lending: Innovation and Technology and the Implications for Regulation," *Harvard Business School Working Paper*, no. 17-042 (2016): 121, http://www.hbs.edu/faculty/Publication%20Files/17-042_30393d52-3c61-41cb-a78a-ebbe3e040e55.pdf.

20. "Small Business Lending Fund," *U.S. Department of the Treasury*, accessed January 19, 2018, https://www.treasury.gov/resource-center/sb-programs/Pages/Small-Business-Lending-Fund.aspx.

21. Kevin T. Jacques, Richard Moylan, and Peter J. Nigro, "Commercial Bank Small Business Lending Pre and Post Crisis," *The Journal of Entrepreneurial Finance* 18, no. 1 (Spring 2016): 22–48, https://digitalcommons.pepperdine.edu/cgi/viewcontent.cgi?referer=&httpsredir=1&article=1275&context=jef.

22. Jeff Zients, "Getting Money to Small Businesses Faster," *The White House Blog*, September 14, 2011, https://www.whitehouse.gov/blog/2011/09/14/getting-money-small-businesses-faster.

23. Jean-Noel Barrot and Ramana Nanda, "The Employment Effects of Faster Payment: Evidence from the Federal Quickpay Reform," *Harvard Business School Working Paper*, no. 17-004, July 2016, (Revised July 2018), https://papers.ssrn.com/sol3/papers.cfm?abstract_id=2808666.

24. Federal News Radio Staff, "Necole Parker, Founder and CEO of The ELOCEN Group LLC," *Federal News Radio*, July 31, 2014, https://federalnewsradio.com/federal-drive/2014/07/necole-parker-founder-and-ceo-of-the-elocen-group-llc/.

25. "Helping Small Business Overcome Barriers to Growth," United States House of Representatives Committee on Small Business, Testimony of Steven H. Strongin, February 14, 2018, https://smallbusiness.house.gov/uploadedfiles/2-14-18_strongin_testimony.pdf.

26. Paul Davidson, "U.S. Economy Regains All Jobs Lost in Recession," *USA Today*, June 6, 2014, https://www.usatoday.com/story/money/business/2014/06/06/may-jobs-report/10037173/.

27. Collin Eaton, "Jamie Dimon Dishes on Small Business Lending, Regulatory Issues," *Houston Business Journal*, February 27, 2013, https://www.bizjournals.com/houston/blog/money-makers/2013/02/dimon-dishes-on-small-business.html.

28. William C. Dunkelberg and Holly Wade, "NFIB Small Business Economic Trends," *National Federation of Independent Business*, June 2012, 18, http://www.nfib.com/Portals/0/PDF/sbet/sbet201206.pdf.

29. Small Business Survey Topline—3rd Qtr 2017," *Wells Fargo and Gallup*, July 19, 2017, p. 8–9, https://assets.ctfassets.net/ewhhtaabqlyo/2ytUTLKjMcM4y4yEMYSMIs/4283c944c34c9345ea9b16bb028f226f/Wells_Fargo_Small_Business_Survey_Q3_2017_FINAL7-19-2017.pdf.

30. Manuel Adelino, Antoinette Schoar, and Felipe Severino, "House Prices, Collateral and Self-Employment," *Journal of Financial Economics* 117, no. 2 (2015): 288–306, https://doi.org/10.1016/j.jfineco.2015.03.005.

31. Karen Gordon Mills and Brayden McCarthy, "The State of Small Business Lending: Credit Access During the Recovery and How Technology May Change the Game," *Harvard Business School Working Paper*, no. 15-004 (2014): 30, http://www.hbs.edu/faculty/Publication%20Files/15-004_09b1bf8b-eb2a-4e63-9c4e-0374f770856f.pdf.

32. "Small Business, Credit Access, and a Lingering Recession," *National Federation of Independent Business*, January 2012, 35, https://www.nfib.com/Portals/0/PDF/AllUsers/research/studies/small-business-credit-study-nfib-2012.pdf.

33. Michael D. Bordo and John V. Duca, "The Impact of the Dodd-Frank Act on Small Business," *NBER Working Paper*, no. 24501, April 2018, www.nber.org/papers/w24501.

34. Martin N. Baily, Justin Schardin, and Phillip L. Swagel, "Did Policymakers Get Post-Crisis Financial Regulation Right?," *Bipartisan Policy Center*, September 2016, https://cdn.bipartisanpolicy.org/wp-content/uploads/2016/09/BPC-FRRI-Post-Crisis-Financial-Regulation.pdf.

35. Steve Strongin, Sandra Lawson, Amanda Hindlian, Katherine Maxwell, Koby Sadan, and Sonya Banerjee, "Who Pays for Bank Regulation?," Goldman Sachs Global Markets Institute, June 2014, https://www.goldmansachs.com/insights/public-policy/regulatory-reform/who-pays-for-bank-regulation-pdf.pdf.

36. Sam Batkins and Dan Goldbeck, "Six Years After Dodd-Frank: Higher Costs, Uncertain Benefits," *American Action Forum*, July 20, 2016, https://www.americanactionforum.org/insight/six-years-dodd-frank-higher-costs-uncertain-benefits/.

37. Llewellyn Hinkes-Jones, "How Much Did Dodd-Frank Cost? Don't Ask Banks," *Bloomberg BNA*, February 2, 2017, https://www.bna.com/doddfrank-cost-dont-n57982083211/.

38. Ron Feldman, Ken Heinecke, and Jason Schmidt, "Quantifying the Costs of Additional Regulation on Community Banks," *Federal Reserve Bank of Minneapolis*, May 30, 2013, https://www.minneapolisfed.org/research/economic-policy-papers/quantifying-the-costs-of-additional-regulation-on-community-banks.

39. Drew Dahl, Andrew Meyer, and Michelle Neely, "Bank Size, Compliance Costs and Compliance Performance in Community Banking," *Federal Reserve Bank of St. Louis*, May 2016, https://www.communitybanking.org/~/media/files/communitybanking/2016/session2_paper2_neely.pdf.

40. "2017 Small Business Credit Survey: Report on Employer Firms," *Federal Reserve Banks*, May 2018, p. 7, https://www.fedsmallbusiness.org/medialibrary/fedsmallbusiness/files/2018/sbcs-employer-firms-report.pdf.

Chapter 4

1. Ruth Simon, "What Happened When a Town Lost Its Only Bank Branch," *The Wall Street Journal*, December 25, 2017, https://www.wsj.com/articles/what-happened-when-a-town-lost-its-only-bank-branch-1514219228.

2. Ann Marie Wiersch and Scott Shane, "Why Small Business Lending Isn't What It Used to Be," *Federal Reserve Bank of Cleveland*, August 14, 2013, https://www.clevelandfed.org/newsroom-and-events/publications/economic-commentary/2013-economic-commentaries/ec-201310-why-small-business-lending-isnt-what-it-used-to-be.aspx.

3. "2017 Small Business Credit Survey: Report on Employer Firms," *Federal Reserve Banks*, May 2018, p. 13, https://www.fedsmallbusiness.org/medialibrary/fedsmallbusiness/files/2018/sbcs-employer-firms-report.pdf.

4. Ibid.

5. Note: Banks with assets from $10 billion to $250 billion, and large banks with assets over $250 billion do provide 67% of small business loans by dollars. No data exists on the number of loans, but the hypothesis is that community banks provide a larger number of small-dollar loans, those under $250,000. Having better data on the number of loans made by size of bank would provide further clarity on the role and importance of community banks.

6. Allen Berger and Gregory Udell, "Relationship Lending and Lines of Credit in Small Firm Finance," *Journal of Business* 68, no. 3 (1995): 351–381, https://scholarcommons.sc.edu/cgi/viewcontent.cgi?article=1009&context=fin_facpub.

7. Jonathan Scott and William Dunkelberg, "Bank Consolidation and Small Business Lending: A Small Firm Perspective," *Proceedings* (1991): 328–361.

8. Brian Uzzi and James Gillespie, "Corporate Social Capital and the Cost of Financial Capital: An Embeddedness Approach," in *Corporate Social Capital and Liability*, eds. R.T.A.J. Leenders and S.M. Gabbay (Boston, MA: Springer, 1999), 446–459.

9. Robert DeYoung, Dennis Glennon, and Peter Nigro, "Borrower-Lender Distance, Credit Scoring, and Loan Performance: Evidence from Informational-Opaque Small Business Borrowers," *Journal of Financial Intermediation* 17, no. 1 (2008): 113–143, https://doi.org/10.1016/j.jfi.2007.07.002.

10. "2015 Small Business Credit Survey: Report on Employer Firms," *Federal Reserve Banks*, March 2016, p. 9, https://www.newyorkfed.org/medialibrary/media/smallbusiness/2015/Report-SBCS-2015.pdf.

11. Ryan N. Banerjee, Leonardo Gambacorta, and Enrico Sette, "The Real Effects of Relationship Lending," *Bank for International Settlements Working Papers*, no. 662, September 2017, https://www.bis.org/publ/work662.pdf.

12. John R. Walter, "Depression-Era Bank Failures: The Great Contagion or the Great Shakeout?," *Federal Reserve Bank of Richmond Economic Quarterly* 91, no. 1 (2005), https://www.richmondfed.org/-/media/richmondfedorg/publications/research/economic_quarterly/2005/winter/pdf/walter.pdf.

13. "Commercial Banks in the U.S.," *FRED Economic Data (Federal Reserve Bank of St. Louis)*, last modified August 16, 2018, https://fred.stlouisfed.org/series/USNUM.

14. "Commercial Banks—Historical Statistics on Banking," *Federal Deposit Insurance Corporation*, accessed September 14, 2018, https://www5.fdic.gov/hsob/SelectRpt.asp?EntryTyp=10&Header=1.

15. "FDIC Community Banking Study," *Federal Deposit Insurance Corporation*, December 2012, pp. 2–4, https://www.fdic.gov/regulations/resources/cbi/report/cbi-full.pdf.
16. Note: A thrift, also known as a savings and loan, specializes in taking deposits for savings, and making loans, especially mortgage loans. Thrifts came into vogue in the United States starting in the 1930s after the passage of the Federal Home Loan Bank Act as a way to allow a greater percentage of Americans to own their homes. Thrifts have become increasingly similar to banks over time.
17. Kevin J. Stiroh and Jennifer P. Poole, "Explaining the Rising Concentration of Banking Assets in the 1990s," *Current Issues in Economics and Finance* 6, no. 9, August 2000, https://pdfs.semanticscholar.org/5b0b/6879f388106468e74380414b60a9a565a4f4.pdf.
18. "FDIC Community Banking Study," *Federal Deposit Insurance Corporation*, December 2012, pp. I–II, https://www.fdic.gov/regulations/resources/cbi/report/cbi-full.pdf.
19. *Supervisory Insights* 13, no. 1 (Summer 2016): 3, https://www.fdic.gov/regulations/examinations/supervisory/insights/sisum16/si_summer16.pdf.
20. Andrew Martin, "In Hard Times, One New Bank (Double-Wide)," *New York Times*, August 2010, http://www.nytimes.com/2010/08/29/business/29bank.html.
21. John J. Maxfield, "The New Crop of De Novo Banks," *BankDirector.com*, April 5, 2017, http://www.bankdirector.com/magazine/archives/2nd-quarter-2017/new-crop-de-novo-banks; Note: This may underestimate the actual influx of new banks as the FDIC did encourage new entrants to buy the charters of troubled banks, with some positive results.
22. Yan Lee and Chiwon Yom, "The Entry, Performance, and Risk Profile of De Novo Banks," *FDIC-CFR Working Paper*, no. 2016-03 (April 2016), https://www.fdic.gov/bank/analytical/cfr/2016/wp2016/2016-03.pdf.
23. Jeff Bater, "Low Interest Rates to Blame for Few Bank Startups, FDIC Says," *Bloomberg Law Banking*, July 14, 2016, https://www.bna.com/low-interest-rates-n73014444685/.
24. Charles S. Morris and Kristen Regehr, "What Explains Low Net Interest Income at Community Banks?," Consolidated Reports of Condition and Income, https://www.communitybankingconnections.org/articles/2015/q2/what-explains-low-net-interest-income.
25. "FDIC Community Banking Study," *Federal Deposit Insurance Corporation*, December 2012, pp. III–IV, https://www.fdic.gov/regulations/resources/cbi/report/cbi-full.pdf.
26. Ruth Simon and Coulter Jones, "Goodbye, George Bailey: Decline of Rural Lending Crimps Small-Town Business," *The Wall Street Journal*,

December 25, 2017, https://www.wsj.com/articles/goodbye-george-bailey-decline-of-rural-lending-crimps-small-town-business-1514219515.

27. Hoai-Luu Q. Nguyen, "Do Bank Branches Still Matter? The Effect of Closings on Local Economic Outcomes," MIT Economics, December 2014, http://economics.mit.edu/files/10143.

28. Ibid.

29. Oliver E. Williamson, "Hierarchical Control and Optimum Firm Size," *Journal of Political Economy* 75, no. 2 (April 1927): 123–138, https://www.journals.uchicago.edu/doi/10.1086/259258.

30. Rebel A. Cole, Lawrence G. Goldberg, and Lawrence J. White, "Cookie Cutter vs. Character: The Micro Structure of Small Business Lending by Large and Small Banks," *Journal of Financial and Quantitative Analysis* 39, no. 2 (June 2004): 227–251, https://condor.depaul.edu/rcole/Research/Cole.Goldberg.White.JFQA.2004.pdf.

31. "Small Business Lending Survey," *FDIC*, November 1, 2017, https://www.fdic.gov/communitybanking/2017/2017-11-01-sbls.pdf.

32. John H. Cushman, Jr., "Credit Markets; Secondary Market Is Sought," *New York Times*, March 29, 1993, http://www.nytimes.com/1993/03/29/business/credit-markets-secondary-market-is-sought.html?mcubz=3.

33. Kenneth Temkin and Roger C. Kormendi, "An Exploration of a Secondary Market for Small Business Loans," *Small Business Administration Office of Advocacy*, April 2003, 12–13, http://citeseerx.ist.psu.edu/viewdoc/download?doi=10.1.1.186.8863&rep=rep1&type=pdf.

34. "Fall 2013 Small Business Credit Survey," *Federal Reserve Bank of New York*, September 2013, https://www.newyorkfed.org/medialibrary/interactives/fall2013/fall2013/files/full-report.pdf.

Chapter 5

1. Karen Gordon Mills and Brayden McCarthy, "The State of Small Business Lending: Credit Access during the Recovery and How Technology May Change the Game," *Harvard Business School Working Paper*, no. 15-004 (2014), http://www.hbs.edu/faculty/Publication%20Files/15-004_09b1bf8b-eb2a-4e63-9c4e-0374f770856f.pdf.

2. Note: The variation in the data may be due to differences in the types of small businesses sampled or in the way the questions about accessing credit were asked.

3. Jacob Jegher and Ian Benton, "Build, Buy, Partner, and Beyond: How Alternative Lending is Reshaping Small Business Lending," *Javelin Strategy*, May 16, 2016, https://www.javelinstrategy.com/coverage-area/%E2%80%98build-buy-or-partner%E2%80%99-and-beyond.

4. "2017 Small Business Credit Survey: Report on Employer Firms," *Federal Reserve Banks*, May 2018, p. 6, https://www.fedsmallbusiness.org/medialibrary/fedsmallbusiness/files/2018/sbcs-employer-firms-report.pdf.

5. "2016 Small Business Credit Survey: Report on Employer Firms," *Federal Reserve Banks*, April 2017, p. 12, https://www.newyorkfed.org/medialibrary/media/smallbusiness/2016/SBCS-Report-EmployerFirms-2016.pdf.

6. "Joint Small Business Credit Survey Report 2014," Federal Reserve Banks of New York, Atlanta, Cleveland and Philadelphia, 2014, p. 6. https://www.newyorkfed.org/medialibrary/media/smallbusiness/SBCS-2014-Report.pdf.

7. "2016 Small Business Credit Survey: Report on Startup Firms," *Federal Reserve Banks*, August 2017, https://www.newyorkfed.org/medialibrary/media/smallbusiness/2016/SBCS-Report-StartupFirms-2016.pdf.

8. "2016 Small Business Credit Survey: Report on Startup Firms," *Federal Reserve Banks*, August 2017, p. 7, https://www.newyorkfed.org/medialibrary/media/smallbusiness/2016/SBCS-Report-StartupFirms-2016.pdf.

9. Ruth Simon and Paul Overberg, "Funding Sources Shift for Startups," *Wall Street Journal*, September 28, 2016, http://www.wsj.com/articles/funding-sources-shift-for-startups-1475095802?tesla=y.

10. Interview with Linda Pagan, August 2, 2018.

11. Note: The SBA has a portfolio of nearly $100 billion of guarantees, with a loss rate of less than 5 percent, indicating that there is a significant set of worthy small businesses in the market that might not otherwise qualify for loans. Since the cost of the losses is generally covered by SBA fees, the federal budget impact of this significant program is close to zero. The program is a great example of a public-private partnership that takes advantage of bank expertise to provide more access and opportunity for small businesses at little government expense. This is a useful model to consider for other market gaps or social purposes, and the program has been copied by other nations in order to better support their small business sectors.

Chapter 6

1. Michael Riordan and Lillian Hoddeson, *Crystal Fire: The Invention of the Transistor* (W. W. Norton, 1997), 254.

2. Joseph Alois Schumpeter, *Business Cycles* (New York: McGraw-Hill, 1939).

3. Joseph Schumpeter, *Capitalism, Socialism and Democracy* (New York: Routledge, 2010), 83.

4. Joseph Alois Schumpeter, *The Theory of Economic Development: An Inquiry into Profits, Capital, Credit, Interest, and the Business Cycle* (New Brunswick, NJ: Transaction Books, 1911), 66.

5. Rebecca Henderson, "Developing and Managing a Successful Technology & Product Strategy: The Industry Life Cycle as an S Curve," The Co-Evolution of Technologies and Markets, Cambridge, MA, 2005, www.mit.edu/people/rhenders/Teaching/day1_jan05.ppt.

6. Priya Ganapati, "June 4, 1977: VHS Comes to America," *Wired*, June 4, 2010, https://www.wired.com/2010/06/0604vhs-ces/.

7. "Check Clearing for the 21st Century Act (Check 21)," *Federal Deposit Insurance Corporation*, last modified April 3, 2017, https://www.fdic.gov/consumers/assistance/protection/check21.html.

8. "FDIC Quarterly Banking Profile," *Federal Deposit Insurance Corporation*, accessed September 14, 2018, https://www.fdic.gov/bank/analytical/qbp/.

9. Brian Riley, "Small Business Credit Cards Have Plenty of Growth Potential in the U.S.," *Mercator Advisory Group*, March 14, 2018, https://www.mercatoradvisorygroup.com/Templates/BlogPost.aspx?id=6866&blogid=25506.

10. "FDIC Quarterly Banking Profile," *Federal Deposit Insurance Corporation*, accessed September 14, 2018, https://www.fdic.gov/bank/analytical/qbp/.

11. "Total Consumer Credit Owned and Securitized, Outstanding," *FRED Economic Data*, accessed March 23, 2018, https://fred.stlouisfed.org/graph/?id=TOTALSL.

12. "Real Estate Loans: Residential Real Estate Loans, All Commercial Banks," *FRED Economic Data*, https://fred.stlouisfed.org/graph/?id=RREACBW027SBOG.

13. "Annual Report 2017," JPMorgan Chase & Co., April 2018, p. 14, https://www.jpmorganchase.com/corporate/investor-relations/document/annualreport-2017.pdf.

14. Parris Sanz, "CAN Capital Celebrates 20 Years," *CAN Capital*, March 21, 2018, https://www.cancapital.com/resources/can-capital-celebrates-20-years/.

15. Rip Empson, "Smart Lending: On Deck Gives Your Startup a Credit Score So You Can Secure a Loan," *TechCrunch*, May 19, 2011, https://techcrunch.com/2011/05/19/smart-lending-on-deck-gives-your-startup-a-credit-score-so-you-can-secure-a-loan/.

16. Karen Gordon Mills and Brayden McCarthy, "The State of Small Business Lending: Innovation and Technology and the Implications for Regulation," *Harvard Business School Working Paper*, no. 17-042, 2016, http://www.hbs.edu/faculty/Publication%20Files/17-042_30393d52-3c61-41cb-a78a-ebbe3e040e55.pdf.

17. Michael Erman and Joy Wiltermuth, "Lending Club CEO Resigns After Internal Probe, Shares Plummet," *Reuters*, May 9, 2016, https://www.reuters.com/article/us-lendingclub-results-idUSKCN0Y01BK.

18. Leena Rao, "Once-Hot Online Lending Companies Go Cold in Face of Skepticism," *Fortune*, July 1, 2015, http://fortune.com/2015/06/30/lending-club-ondeck-shares/.

19. Kristine McKenna, "Lots of Aura, No Air Play," *Los Angeles Times*, May 23, 1982, L6.

Chapter 7

1. LendIt Archives, Courtesy of Peter Renton, accessed March 13, 2018.

2. "LendIt 2013 Official Conference Report," *LendIt Blog*, August 24, 2013, http://blog.lendit.com/lendit-2013-official-conference-report/.

3. Peter Renton, "Wrap-Up of the 2014 LendIt Conference," *Lend Academy*, May 9, 2014, https://www.lendacademy.com/wrap-up-of-the-2014-lendit-conference/.

4. "The LendIt Story," *Lendit Conference*, 2018, http://www.lendit.com/about.

5. "LendIt USA 2015: Agenda at a Glance," *Lendit USA*, 2015, https://s3-us-west-2.amazonaws.com/lendit/agendas/usa-2015-agenda.pdf.

6. Travis Skelly, "Larry Summers' Full-throated Endorsement of Online Lending," *FinTech Collective*, April 16, 2015, http://news.fintech.io/post/102ceyr/larry-summers-full-throated-endorsement-of-online-lending.

7. Interview with Frank Rotman, April 13, 2018.

8. Rolin Zumeran, "The History of APIs and How They Impact Your Future," *OpenLegacy Blog*, June 7, 2017, http://www.openlegacy.com/blog/the-history-of-apis-and-how-they-impact-your-future.

9. "Open Banking's Next Wave: Perspectives from Three Fintech CEOs," *Business a.m.*, September 10, 2018, https://www.businessamlive.com/open-bankings-next-wave-perspectives-from-three-fintech-ceos/.

10. Parris Sanz, "CAN Capital Celebrates 20 Years," *CAN Capital*, March 21, 2018, https://www.cancapital.com/resources/can-capital-celebrates-20-years/.

11. Note: APR refers to an Annual Percentage Rate, or what most think of as an "interest rate." This number represents the percent interest paid on a loan over the course of a year. Because MCAs are repaid using a percentage of a business's sales receipts, they could be repaid in a shorter timeframe than a year. However, since the repayment amount is fixed, the calculation of APR can be quite high if the loan is repaid in a short time

frame. As a result, some argue that APRs unfairly represent the true cost of MCA loans. Nonetheless, APRs remain the standard for interest rate disclosures and comparisons.

12. Jackson Mueller, "U.S. Online, Non-Bank Finance Landscape," *Milken Institute Center for Financial Markets*, Curated through May 2016, http://www.milkeninstitute.org/assets/PDF/Online-Non-Bank-Finance-Landscape.pdf.

13. "Lending Club Launches Business Loans," *LendingClub*, accessed March 27, 2018, https://blog.lendingclub.com/lending-club-launches-business-loans/.

14. Julapa Jagtiani and Catharine Lemieux, "Small Business Lending: Challenges and Opportunities for Community Banks," *Philadelphia Fed Working Paper*, no. 16-08 (March 2016), https://philadelphiafed.org/-/media/research-and-data/publications/working-papers/2016/wp16-08.pdf.

15. Kabbage, accessed September 17, 2018, https://www.kabbage.com/.

16. Interview with Kathryn Petralia, March 19, 2018.

17. Miranda Eifler, "The OnDeck Score: Making Targeted Small Business Lending Decisions in Real Time," accessed March 27, 2018, https://www.ondeck.com/resources/ondeckscore.

18. Jackson Mueller, "U.S. Online, Non-Bank Finance Landscape," *Milken Institute Center for Financial Markets*, Curated through May 2016, http://www.milkeninstitute.org/assets/PDF/Online-Non-Bank-Finance-Landscape.pdf.

19. OnDeck, accessed April 18, 2018, https://www.ondeck.com/company.

20. Interview with Peter Renton, March 28, 2018.

21. Peter Renton, "Funding Circle Raises $37 Million and Launches in The U.S.," *Lend Academy*, October 23, 2013, https://www.lendacademy.com/funding-circle-raises-37-million-and-launches-in-the-u-s/.

22. Allen Taylor, "Will Amazon Lending Disrupt, Displace, or Prop Up Banks?" *Lending Times*, January 4, 2018, https://lending-times.com/2018/01/04/will-amazon-lending-disrupt-displace-or-prop-up-banks/.

23. Jeffrey Dastin, "Amazon Lent $1 Billion to Merchants to Boost Sales on Its Marketplace," *Reuters*, June 8, 2017, https://www.reuters.com/article/us-amazon-com-loans-idUSKBN18Z0DY.

24. Amy Feldman, "PayPal's Small-Business Lending Tops $3B As Company Launches New Tools For Small-Business Owners," *Forbes*, May 1, 2017, https://www.forbes.com/sites/amyfeldman/2017/05/01/paypals-small-business-lending-tops-3b-as-company-launches-new-tools-for-small-business-owners/#7a8014b34018.

25. Leena Rao, "Square Capital Has Loaned Over $1 Billion to Small Businesses," *Fortune*, November 7, 2016, http://fortune.com/2016/11/07/square-capital-1-billion/.

26. "Q2 2018 Shareholder Letter," *Square*, p. 7, https://s21.q4cdn.com/114365585/files/doc_financials/2018/2018-Q2-Shareholder-Letter-%E2%80%94-Square.pdf.

27. Note: As described in Chapter 2, small supply chain firms account for almost 1 million small businesses and about 10 million jobs, with high average wages and significant amounts of innovation.

28. Note: In April 2018, Orchard was acquired by Kabbage, helping Kabbage gain access to Orchard's data science technology, https://www.kabbage.com/pdfs/pressreleases/Kabbage_Acquire_Orchard.pdf.

29. Author's analysis and data from "Breaking New Ground: The Americas Alternative Finance Benchmarking Report," *Cambridge Centre for Alternative Finance*, 2016, https://www.jbs.cam.ac.uk/fileadmin/user_upload/research/centres/alternative-finance/downloads/2016-americas-alternative-finance-benchmarking-report.pdf.

30. "Global Marketplace Lending: Disruptive Innovation in Financials," *Morgan Stanley*, May 19, 2015, https://bebeez.it/wp-content/blogs.dir/5825/files/2015/06/GlobalMarketplaceLending.pdf.

31. "Fintech Investment in U.S. Nearly Tripled in 2014, According to Report by Accenture and Partnership Fund for New York City," *Accenture*, June 25, 2015, https://newsroom.accenture.com/news/fintech-investment-in-us-nearly-tripled-in-2014-according-to-report-by-accenture-and-partnership-fund-for-new-york-city.htm.

32. Geoffrey A. Moore, *Crossing the Chasm: Marketing and Selling Disruptive Products to Mainstream Customers* (HarperBusiness Essentials, 2002), 9, http://library.globalchalet.net/Authors/Startup%20Collection/%5BMoore,%202002%5D%20Crossing%20the%20Chasm,%20Revised%20Edition.pdf.

33. Geoffrey A. Moore, *Inside the Tornado: Strategies for Developing, Leveraging, and Surviving Hypergrowth Markets* (HarperCollins Publishers, 2009), 26, https://docslide.us/documents/inside-the-tornado-geoffrey-a-moore.html.

34. Securities and Exchange Commission, Form 10-K: OnDeck Capital Inc., 2015, http://d1lge852tjjqow.cloudfront.net/CIK-0001420811/2e36150d-a925-4b94-ad17-1d111b90ba94.pdf; "Lending Club Reports Fourth Quarter and Full Year 2015 Results and Announces $150 Million Share Buyback," *PRNewswire*, February 11, 2016, http://www.prnewswire.com/news-releases/lending-club-reports-fourth-quarter-and-full-year-2015-results-and-announces-150-million-share-buyback-300218747.html.

35. Chris Myers, "For Alternative Lenders to Be Successful, Differentiation Is Key," *Forbes*, October 2015, http://www.forbes.com/sites/chrismyers/ 2015/10/15/for-alternative-lenders-to-be-successful-differentiation-is-key/#722f3110207e.

36. Karen Gordon Mills, Dennis Campbell, and Aaron Mukerjee, "Eastern Bank: Innovating Through Eastern Labs," HBS No. 9-318-068 (Boston: Harvard Business School Publishing, 2017), https://www.hbs.edu/faculty/ Pages/item.aspx?num=53399.

Chapter 8

1. Interview with Shivani Siroya of Tala, June 19, 2018.

2. Emma Dunkley, "UK Banks Prepare to Share Customer Data in Radical Shake-up," *Financial Times*, November 26, 2017, https://www.ft.com/ content/55f4503e-cb95-11e7-ab18-7a9fb7d6163e.

3. Bernard Marr, "28 Best Quotes About Artificial Intelligence," *Forbes*, July 25, 2017, https://www.forbes.com/sites/bernardmarr/2017/07/25/28-best-quotes-about-artificial-intelligence/#7f333fbc4a6f.

4. "This Hot Robot Says She Wants to Destroy Humans," *CNBC*, March 16, 2016, https://www.cnbc.com/video/2016/03/16/this-hot-robot-says-she-wants-to-destroy-humans.html.

5. Bernard Marr, "28 Best Quotes About Artificial Intelligence," *Forbes*, July 25, 2017, https://www.forbes.com/sites/bernardmarr/2017/07/25/28-best-quotes-about-artificial-intelligence/#7f333fbc4a6f.

6. Iain M. Cockburn, Rebecca Henderson, and Scott Stern, "The Impact of Artificial Intelligence on Innovation: An Exploratory Analysis," Chapter in forthcoming NBER Book The Economics of Artificial Intelligence: An Agenda, December 16, 2017, http://www.nber.org/chapters/c14006.pdf.

7. Zvi Griliches, "Hybrid Corn: An Exploration in the Economics of Technological Change," *Econometrica* 25, no. 4 (1957): 501–522.

8. "Small Business Development Center," *U.S. Small Business Administration, Local Assistance*, https://www.sba.gov/tools/local-assistance/sbdc.

9. "SCORE Business Mentor," *U.S. Small Business Administration, Local Assistance*, https://www.sba.gov/tools/local-assistance/score.

10. "Community Development Financial Institutions Fund," *U.S. Department of the Treasury*, https://www.cdfifund.gov/Pages/default.aspx.

11. "Chase Initiative Sparks Debate Over 'Bank Deserts' And SMBs," *PYMNTS*, August 21, 2018, https://www.pymnts.com/news/b2b-payments/2018/ jpmorgan-chase-small-business-advisory-banking-branches/.

12. Suman Bhattacharyya, "Chase to Reach Business Owners Through 'Business Advice Center on Wheels'," *Tearsheet*, June 15, 2018, https://www.tearsheet.co/marketing/chase-to-reach-business-owners-through-business-advice-center-on-wheels?utm_source=digiday.com&utm_medium=referral&utm_campaign=digidaydis&utm_content=bhattacharyya-chase-to-reach-business-owners-through-business-advice-center-on-wheels.

Chapter 9

1. For more on this story, see Karen Gordon Mills, Dennis Campbell, and Aaron Mukerjee, "*Eastern Bank: Innovating Through Eastern Labs*," HBS No. 9-318-068 (Boston: Harvard Business School Publishing, 2017), https://www.hbs.edu/faculty/Pages/item.aspx?num=53399; Note: The author is an investor in Numerated Growth Technologies.
2. Peter Rudegeair, Emily Glazer, and Ruth Simon, "Inside J.P. Morgan's Deal with On Deck Capital," *Wall Street Journal*, December 30, 2015, https://www.wsj.com/articles/inside-j-p-morgans-deal-with-on-deck-capital-1451519092.
3. Peter Renton, "An In Depth Look at the OnDeck/JPMorgan Chase Deal," *LendAcademy*, December 4, 2015, https://www.lendacademy.com/an-in-depth-look-at-the-ondeckjpmorgan-chase-deal/.
4. Jonathan Kandell, "Jamie Dimon is Not Messing Around," *Institutional Investor*, May 21, 2018. https://www.institutionalinvestor.com/article/b189czlk410ggh/jamie-dimon-is-not-messing-around.
5. "*FastFlex*® Small Business Loan Calculator," accessed June 26, 2018, https://www.wellsfargo.com/biz/business-credit/loans/fastflex-loan/payment-calculator/.
6. "Wells Fargo Works *for Small Business*®," accessed June 26, 2018, https://wellsfargoworks.com/.
7. Harriet Taylor, "Bank of America Launches AI Chatbot Erica—Here's What It Does," *CNBC*, October 24, 2016, https://www.cnbc.com/2016/10/24/bank-of-america-launches-ai-chatbot-erica%2D%2Dheres-what-it-does.html.
8. "After the dinosaurs," *The Economist*, February 17, 2000, http://www.economist.com/node/284246.
9. "About Us," *Frost Bank*, accessed September 21, 2018, https://www.frostbank.com/about-us.
10. "Community Capital," accessed June 22, 2018, https://www.communitytechnology.us/.

11. "Where Top US Banks are Investing in Fintech—CB Insights," *Fintech Futures*, August 14, 2017, http://www.bankingtech.com/2017/08/where-top-us-banks-are-investing-in-fintech-cb-insights/.

12. "Citizens Bank Makes It Faster, Easier to Get Small Business Loans with New Digital Lending Capability," *Citizens Financial Group, Inc.*, November 2, 2017, http://investor.citizensbank.com/about-us/news-room/latest-news/2017/2017-11-02-110049591.aspx.

13. "Rise," *Barclays PLC*, accessed June 29, 2018, https://thinkrise.com/.

14. Ryan Weeks, "MarketInvoice Strikes Strategic Deal with Barclays," *AltFi*, August 2, 2018, http://www.altfi.com/article/4631_marketinvoice-strikes-strategic-deal-with-barclays.

15. "Citizens Bank Makes It Faster, Easier to Get Small Business Loans with New Digital Lending Capability," *Citizens Financial Group, Inc.*, November 2, 2017, http://investor.citizensbank.com/about-us/news-room/latest-news/2017/2017-11-02-110049591.aspx.

16. "Wells Fargo Labs," accessed March 27, 2018, https://labs.wellsfargo.com/.

17. Note: For a more detailed description of the options in this matrix, see: Karen Mills and Brayden McCarthy, "How Banks Can Compete Against an Army of Fintech Startups," *Harvard Business Review*, April 26, 2017, https://hbr.org/2017/04/how-banks-can-compete-against-an-army-of-fintech-startups.

18. "2016 Small Business Credit Survey: Report on Employer Firms," *Federal Reserve Banks*, April 2017, https://www.newyorkfed.org/medialibrary/media/smallbusiness/2016/SBCS-Report-EmployerFirms-2016.pdf.

19. Michael T. Tushman, Wendy K. Smith, and Andy Binns. "The Ambidextrous CEO," *Harvard Business Review*, June 2011, https://hbr.org/2011/06/the-ambidextrous-ceo; Charles A. O'Reilly and Michael L. Tushman, "The Ambidextrous Organization," *Harvard Business Review*, April 2004, https://hbr.org/2004/04/the-ambidextrous-organization.

20. Shikhar Ghosh, Joseph Fuller, and Michael Roberts. *Intuit: Turbo Tax PersonalPro—A Tale of Two Entrepreneurs* (Harvard Business School: Harvard Business Publishing, Revised 2016), https://www.hbs.edu/faculty/Pages/item.aspx?num=49820.

21. William R. Kerr, Federica Gabrieli, and Emer Moloney, "*Transformation at ING (A): Agile*," HBS No. 9-818-077 (Boston, Harvard Business School Publishing, 2018), https://www.hbs.edu/faculty/Pages/item.aspx?num=53838.

22. Karen Gordon Mills, Dennis Campbell, and Aaron Mukerjee, "*Eastern Bank: Innovating Through Eastern Labs*," HBS No. 9-318-068 (Boston: Harvard Business School Publishing, 2017), https://www.hbs.edu/faculty/Pages/item.aspx?num=53399.

Chapter 10

1. Sandra K. Hoffman and Tracy G. McGinley, *Identity Theft: A Reference Handbook* (ABC-CLIO, 2010), 11.
2. Sean Vanatta, "The Great Chicago Christmas Credit Card Fiasco of 1966: Echoes," *Bloomberg*, December 24, 2012, https://www.bloomberg.com/view/articles/2012-12-24/the-great-chicago-christmas-credit-card-fiasco-of-1966-echoes.
3. "Financial Regulation: Complex and Fragmented Structure Could Be Streamlined to Improve Effectiveness," *United States Government Accountability Office*, February 2016, http://www.gao.gov/assets/680/675400.pdf.
4. Elizabeth F. Brown, "Prior Proposals to Consolidate Federal Financial Regulators," *The Volcker Alliance*, February 14, 2016, https://www.volckeralliance.org/sites/default/files/attachments/Background%20Paper%201_Prior%20Proposals%20to%20Consolidate%20Federal%20Financial%20Regulators.pdf.
5. "About the Federal Reserve System," *Board of Governors of the Federal Reserve System*, last updated March 3, 2017, https://www.federalreserve.gov/aboutthefed/structure-federal-reserve-system.htm.
6. "Who is the FDIC?," *Federal Deposit Insurance Corporation*, accessed March 27, 2018, https://www.fdic.gov/about/learn/symbol/.
7. "About the OCC," *Office of the Comptroller of the Currency*, accessed December 15, 2017, http://www.occ.gov/about/what-we-do/mission/index-about.html.
8. "Opening Remarks of FTC Chairwoman Edith Ramirez FinTech Forum Series: Marketplace Lending," *Federal Trade Commission*, June 9, 2016, https://www.ftc.gov/system/files/documents/public_statements/956043/ramirez_-_fintech_forum_opening_remarks_6-9-16.pdf.
9. Michael E. Gordon and Franca Harris Gutierrez, "The Future Of CFPB Small Business Lending Regulation," *Law360*, May 19, 2016, http://www.law360.com/articles/797135/the-future-of-cfpb-small-business-lending-regulation.
10. Kevin V. Tu, "Regulating the New Cashless World," *Alabama Law Review* 65, no. 1 (2013): 109, accessed March 27, 2018, https://www.law.ua.edu/pubs/lrarticles/Volume%2065/Issue%201/2%20Tu%2077-138.pdf.
11. "Vision 2020 for Fintech and Non-Bank Regulation," *Conference of State Bank Supervisors*, June 7, 2018, https://www.csbs.org/vision2020.
12. "OCC Begins Accepting National Bank Charter Applications From Financial Technology Companies," *Office of the Comptroller of the*

Currency, July 31, 2018, https://www.occ.gov/news-issuances/news-releases/2018/nr-occ-2018-74.html.

13. "Third-Party Relationships," *Office of the Comptroller of the Currency*, OCC Bulletin 2013–29, October 30, 2013, https://www.occ.gov/news-issuances/bulletins/2013/bulletin-2013-29.html.

14. "Description: Frequently Asked Questions to Supplement OCC Bulletin 2013–29," *Office of the Comptroller of the Currency*, OCC Bulletin 2017–21, June 7, 2017, https://www.occ.treas.gov/news-issuances/bulletins/2017/bulletin-2017-21.html.

15. "Examination Guidance for Third-Party Lending," *Federal Deposit Insurance Corporation*, July 29, 2016, https://www.fdic.gov/news/news/financial/2016/fil16050a.pdf.

16. Steven T. Mnuchin and Craig S. Phillips, "A Financial System That Creates Economic Opportunities: Nonbank Financials, Fintech, and Innovation," *U.S. Department of the Treasury*, July 2018, https://home.treasury.gov/sites/default/files/2018-07/A-Financial-System-that-Creates-Economic-Opportunities%2D%2D-Nonbank-Financi...pdf.

17. Barbara J. Lipman and Ann Marie Wiersch, "Alternative Lending Through the Eyes of 'Mom & Pop' Small-Business Owners: Findings from Online Focus Groups," *Federal Reserve Bank of Cleveland*, August 25, 2015, https://www.clevelandfed.org/newsroom-and-events/publications/special-reports/sr-20150825-alternative-lending-through-the-eyes-of-mom-and-pop-small-business-owners.aspx.

18. Barbara J. Lipman and Ann Marie Wiersch, "Browsing to Borrow: Mom & Pop Small Business Perspectives on Online Lenders," *Federal Reserve Board and Federal Reserve Bank of Cleveland*, June 2018, https://www.federalreserve.gov/publications/files/2018-small-business-lending.pdf.

19. "Unaffordable and Unsustainable: The New Business Lending on Main Street," *Opportunity Fund*, May 2016, http://www.opportunityfund.org/assets/docs/Unaffordable%20and%20Unsustainable-The%20New%20Business%20Lending%20on%20Main%20Street_Opportunity%20Fund%20Research%20Report_May%202016.pdf.

20. Patrick Clark, "How Much is Too Much to Pay for a Small Business Loan," *Bloomberg*, May 16, 2014, http://www.bloomberg.com/news/articles/2014-05-16/how-much-is-too-much-to-pay-for-a-small-business-loan.

21. Ben Wieder, "Even Finance Whizzes Say It's Impossible to Compare Online Small Business Loan Options," *McClatchy*, June 8, 2018, http://www.mcclatchydc.com/news/nation-world/national/article212491199.html.

22. Barbara J. Lipman and Ann Marie Wiersch, "Browsing to Borrow: Mom & Pop Small Business Perspectives on Online Lenders," *Federal Reserve Board and Federal Reserve Bank of Cleveland*, June 2018, https://www.federalreserve.gov/publications/files/2018-small-business-lending.pdf.

23. Patrick Clark, "Forget the Algorithms. Get Me a Loan Broker!," *Bloomberg*, April 4, 2014, https://www.bloomberg.com/news/articles/2014-04-03/alternative-lenders-still-rely-on-loan-brokers.

24. Leonard J. Kennedy, "Memorandum to Chief Executive Officers of Financial Institutions under Section 1071 of the Dodd-Frank Act," *Consumer Financial Protection Bureau*, April 11, 2011, http://files.consumerfinance.gov/f/2011/04/GC-letter-re-1071.pdf.

25. Consumer Financial Protection Bureau, "Request for Information Regarding the Small Business Lending Market," *Federal Register*, May 15, 2017, https://www.federalregister.gov/documents/2017/05/15/2017-09732/request-for-information-regarding-the-small-business-lending-market.

26. Paul Greig, Karen Mills, Olympia Snowe, and Mark Walsh, "Main Street Matters: Ideas for Improving Small Business Financing," *Bipartisan Policy Center*, August 2018, https://bipartisanpolicy.org/wp-content/uploads/2018/07/Main-Street-Matters-Ideas-for-Improving-Small-Business-Financing.pdf.

27. Liz Farmer, "Are Predatory Business Loans the Next Credit Crisis?," *Governing*, May 2015, http://www.governing.com/topics/finance/gov-predatory-business-loans-crisis.html.

28. Brayden McCarthy, "It's Time to Rein in Shady Small Business Loan Brokers," *Forbes*, September 17, 2014, http://www.forbes.com/sites/groupthink/2014/09/17/its-time-to-rein-in-shady-small-business-loan-brokers/#1b7cb26972b7.

Chapter 11

1. Gwendy Donaker Brown and Gabriel Villarreal, "New and Improved: The Small Business Borrower's Bill of Rights," *Opportunity Fund*, April 19, 2017, https://www.opportunityfund.org/media/blog/new-and-improved-the-small-business-borrower%E2%80%99s-bill-of-rights/.

2. "The Small Business Borrowers' Bill of Rights," *Responsible Business Lending Coalition*, accessed September 22, 2018, http://www.borrowers-billofrights.org/.

3. "The SMART Box™ Model Disclosure Initiative," *Innovative Lending Platform Association*, accessed June 26, 2018, http://innovativelending.org/smart-box/.

4. Interview with George Osborne, September 2016.
5. "About the FCA," *Financial Conduct Authority*, accessed March 30, 2018, https://www.fca.org.uk/about/the-fca.
6. "Regulatory Sandbox," *Financial Conduct Authority*, accessed March 30, 2018, https://www.fca.org.uk/firms/regulatory-sandbox.
7. Note: These modifications would apply as long as the waiver or modification did not conflict with FCA objectives or violate U.K. or international law.
8. "Project Innovate and Innovation Hub," *Financial Conduct Authority*, accessed March 30, 2018, https://www.fca.org.uk/firms/fca-innovate.
9. "Regulatory Sandbox Lessons Learned Report," *Financial Conduct Authority*, October 2017, https://www.fca.org.uk/publication/research-and-data/regulatory-sandbox-lessons-learned-report.pdf.
10. Rowland Manthorpe, "What is Open Banking and PSD2? WIRED Explains," *WIRED*, April 17, 2018, https://www.wired.co.uk/article/open-banking-cma-psd2-explained.
11. "Open Banking Standard," *Payment Systems Regulator; Payments Strategy Forum*, https://www.paymentsforum.uk/sites/default/files/documents/Background%20Document%20No.%202%20-%20The%20Open%20Banking%20Standard%20-%20Full%20Report.pdf.
12. Martin Chorzempa, "P2P Series Part 1: Peering Into China's Growing Peer-to-Peer Lending Market," *Peterson Institute for International Economics*, June 27, 2016, https://piie.com/blogs/china-economic-watch/p2p-series-part-1-peering-chinas-growing-peer-peer-lending-market.
13. Joseph Luc Ngai, John Qu, Nicole Zhou, Xiao Liu, Joshua Lan, Xiyuan Fang, Feng Han, and Vera Chen, "Disruption and Connection: Cracking the Myths of China Internet Finance Innovation," *McKinsey Greater China FIG Practice*, July 2016, https://www.mckinsey.com/~/media/mckinsey/industries/financial%20services/our%20insights/whats%20next%20for%20chinas%20booming%20fintech%20sector/disruption-and-connection-cracking-the-myths-of-china-internet-finance-innovation.ashx.
14. (Robin) Hui Huang, "Online P2P Lending and Regulatory Responses in China: Opportunities and Challenges," *Centre for Financial Regulation & Economic Development*, May 8, 2018, https://papers.ssrn.com/sol3/papers.cfm?abstract_id=2991993.
15. Martin Chorzempa, "P2P Series Part 3: China's Online Lending Consolidates As Market Grows," *Peterson Institute for International Economics*, October 12, 2017, https://piie.com/blogs/china-economic-watch/p2p-series-part-3-chinas-online-lending-consolidates-market-grows.

16. Sidney Leng, "One Third of China's 3,000 Peer-to-Peer Lending Platforms 'Problematic': New Report," *South China Morning Post*, September 24, 2016, http://www.scmp.com/news/hong-kong/economy/article/2022317/one-third-chinas-3000-peer-peer-lending-platforms-problematic.

17. Matthew Miller, "Leader of China's $9 Billion Ezubao Online Scam Gets Life; 26 Jailed," *Reuters*, September 12, 2017, https://www.reuters.com/article/us-china-fraud/leader-of-chinas-9-billion-ezubao-online-scam-gets-life-26-jailed-idUSKCN1BN0J6.

18. Neil Gough, "Online Lender Ezubao Took $7.6 Billion in Ponzi Scheme, China Says," *New York Times*, February 1, 2016, https://www.nytimes.com/2016/02/02/business/dealbook/ezubao-china-fraud.html.

19. (Robin) Hui Huang, "Online P2P Lending and Regulatory Responses in China: Opportunities and Challenges," *Centre for Financial Regulation & Economic Development*, May 8, 2018, https://papers.ssrn.com/sol3/papers.cfm?abstract_id=2991993.

20. Leng Cheng, "Quick Take: China to Improve Oversight of Peer-to-Peer Lending," *Caixin*, August 28, 2017, https://www.caixinglobal.com/2017-08-28/101136810.html.

21. Martin Chorzempa, "P2P Series Part 1: Peering Into China's Growing Peer-to-Peer Lending Market," *Peterson Institute for International Economics*, June 27, 2016, https://piie.com/blogs/china-economic-watch/p2p-series-part-1-peering-chinas-growing-peer-peer-lending-market.

22. David Meyer, "Jack Ma's Chinese Fintech Firm Just Raised So Much Money It's Now Worth More Than Goldman Sachs," *Fortune*, June 8, 2018, http://fortune.com/2018/06/08/ant-financial-alipay-14-billion-funding/.

23. Matthew Wong, "China's New Fintech Empires," *CB Insights Future of Fintech Conference*, New York, NY, June 20–21, 2018, https://www.cbinsights.com/reports/FoF_2018_FinancialServicesinChina_Vignette.pdf?utm_campaign=FoF18&utm_campaign=FoF18&utm_source=hs_email&utm_source=hs_email&utm_medium=email&utm_medium=email&_hsenc=p2ANqtz-8jQ1RXnbV60GDuCwW59FlZ-kXngHFRn29Vr3VaxYkz3hGoVFF4Dcur_S31z8O9XXIC1aM1t&utm_content=64002117&_hsenc=p2ANqtz%2D%2Dh_aipQH-ls9_58J-GQDjFizf1dIyJcKIKwWISCGOQfN3nG3-tIqb951VMy34uIof2UieV6r wNSA9qtKTFhuMAXNlnFA&_hsmi=64002117.

24. Stella Yifan Xie, "Jack Ma's Giant Financial Startup is Shaking the Chinese Banking System; Ant Financial is Transforming How Chinese Run Their Daily Finances, Drawing Flak from Big Banks and Warning Shots from the Government," *Wall Street Journal*, July 29, 2018, https://www.wsj.

com/articles/jack-mas-giant-financial-startup-is-shaking-the-chinese-banking-system-1532885367.

25. Raghuram Rajan and Luigi Zingales, *Saving Capitalism from the Capitalists* (New York: Crown Business, 2003), 1.

26. "Sound Practices, Implications of Fintech Developments for Banks and Bank Supervisors," *Bank for International Settlements: Basel Committee on Banking Supervision*, accessed July 2, 2018, https://www.bis.org/bcbs/publ/d431.pdf.

27. "As Fintech Evolves, Can Financial Services Innovation Be Compliant?," *EY*, 2017, https://www.ey.com/Publication/vwLUAssets/ey-the-emergence-and-impact-of-regulatory-sandboxes-in-uk-and-across-apac/$FILE/ey-the-emergence-and-impact-of-regulatory-sandboxes-in-uk-and-across-apac.pdf.

28. "Recommendations and Decisions for Implementing a Responsible Innovation Framework," *Office of the Comptroller of the Currency*, October 2016, pp. 4–5. https://morningconsult.com/wp-content/uploads/2016/10/2016-135a.pdf.

29. Brenna Goth, "Arizona Becomes First Sandbox State for Fintech Products," *Bloomberg BNA*, March 22, 2018, https://www.bna.com/arizona-becomes-first-n57982090236/.

30. James M. Lacko and Janis K. Pappalardo, "Improving Consumer Mortgage Disclosures: An Empirical Assessment of Current and Prototype Disclosure Forms: A Bureau of Economics Staff Report," *Federal Trade Commission*, June 2007, https://www.ftc.gov/reports/improving-consumer-mortgage-disclosures-empirical-assessment-current-prototype-disclosure.

31. Note: The 1968 Truth in Lending Act (TILA) provides strong protections for consumer borrowers by requiring lenders to disclose terms and costs. TILA applies to banks and fintech lenders that make consumer loans, but does not apply to small business borrowers. There are other laws, such as the Equal Credit Opportunity Act (ECOA), which guarantees non-discrimination and applies to any borrower whether they are interacting with a bank or nonbank lender. The operating principle of TILA should be expanded to follow that of ECOA, providing equal protections to both small businesses and consumers when they borrow, regardless of the source of their loans.

32. Note: Industry players have made recommendations on what these regulations might look like through the Small Business Lending Subgroup of the CSBS Fintech Industry Advisory Panel, https://www.csbs.org/csbs-fintech-industry-advisory-panel.

33. Richard H. Neiman and Mark Olson, "Dodd-Frank's Missed Opportunity: A Road Map for a More Effective Regulatory Architecture," *Bipartisan Policy Center*, April 2014, http://bipartisanpolicy.org/wp-content/uploads/sites/default/files/BPC%20Dodd-Frank%20Missed%20Opportunity.pdf.

34. Steven T. Mnuchin and Craig S. Phillips, "A Financial System That Creates Economic Opportunities: Nonbank Financials, Fintech, and Innovation," *U.S. Department of the Treasury*, July 2018, https://home.treasury.gov/sites/default/files/2018-07/A-Financial-System-that-Creates-Economic-Opportunities%2D%2D-Nonbank-Financi...pdf.

35. Richard H. Neiman and Mark Olson, "Dodd-Frank's Missed Opportunity: A Road Map for a More Effective Regulatory Architecture," *Bipartisan Policy Center*, April 2014, http://bipartisanpolicy.org/wp-content/uploads/sites/default/files/BPC%20Dodd-Frank%20Missed%20Opportunity.pdf.

Chapter 12

1. William Goetzmann, *Money Changes Everything: How Finance Made Civilization Possible* (Princeton, NJ: Princeton University Press, 2016), 50.

2. Note: All estimates are merely guesswork, but if 13 percent of small businesses are seeking capital (Chapter 5), an improvement of 5 percent in the number of businesses funded would mean 187,500 additional creditworthy businesses served by the market. The 5 percent estimate stems from the level of the Small Business Administration (SBA) loan portfolio as a percent of the total market, assuming SBA is a proxy for the market gap. SBA's loan portfolio runs between 5 and 10 percent of the market, only guarantees loans that banks would not make under market conditions, and has less than a 5 percent loss rate.

3. Frank Rotman, "The Copernican Revolution in Banking," *QED Investors*, April 8, 2018, https://s3.amazonaws.com/qed-uploads/The+Copernican+Revolution+in+Banking+-+Publication+Version.pdf.

4. Note: The mortgage lending environment leading up to the financial crisis is an example of where lenders' incentives were not aligned with full disclosure of terms or the best interests of their borrowers.

5. Interview with Jack Dorsey at Harvard Business School, March 12, 2014, https://www.thecrimson.com/article/2014/3/18/an-afternoon-with-jack/.

6. Interview with Eric Groves, July 18, 2018; "About Alignable," Accessed December 3, 2018, https://www.alignable.com/about; Note: The author is an investor in Alignable.

7. H.R. 4173 (111th): Dodd-Frank Wall Street Reform and Consumer Protection Act—Section 1071, https://www.govtrack.us/congress/bills/111/hr4173/text.

8. Anastasia Santoreneos, "FinTech Aus Calls on Parliament to Pass Consumer-friendly Laws," *Money Management*, August 17, 2018, https://www.moneymanagement.com.au/news/financial-planning/fintech-aus-calls-parliament-pass-consumer-friendly-laws.

9. Ross Levine, "Financial Development and Economic Growth: Views and Agenda," *Journal of Economic Literature* 35, no. 2 (June 1997): 688–726, https://www.jstor.org/stable/2729790.

10. "About Us," *When Pigs Fly Bakery*, accessed September 23, 2018, https://sendbread.com/about-us/.

Index[1]

---

[1] Note: Page numbers followed by 'n' refer to notes.

© The Author(s) 2018
K. G. Mills, *Fintech, Small Business & the American Dream*,
https://doi.org/10.1007/978-3-030-03620-1